THE ESSENTIAL GUIDE TO
Irish Dance

MARIE DUFFY PASK

THE ESSENTIAL GUIDE TO
Irish Dance

MARIE DUFFY PASK

THE CROWOOD PRESS

First published in 2022 by
The Crowood Press Ltd
Ramsbury, Marlborough
Wiltshire SN8 2HR

enquiries@crowood.com

www.crowood.com

British Library Cataloguing-in-Publication Data
A catalogue record for this book is available from the British Library.

ISBN 978 0 7198 4073 9

Typeset by Simon and Sons
Cover design by Maggie Mellett
Printed and bound in India by Parksons Graphics Pvt Ltd

CONTENTS

FOREWORD

When Marie Duffy told me she was writing a book on the A-Z of Irish dance, I knew that she would be the only person in the world that could do this! Her involvement and true dedication to the teaching and progression of Irish dance from competition to performance, from pastime to professional, makes her the undisputed expert on all things Irish dance.

She has worked alongside me for the past twenty-five years and it has always been a pleasure. What has been refreshing for me has been Marie's in-depth understanding of the evolution of a dancer from amateur to professional, a more complex transition than it may seem, and until the late 1990s was not an option for most. Her expertise and willingness to embrace all the possibilities for a dancer to become the best they can be, is a dream we have both shared for the next generation of dancers. At a time in the world where nobody believed in my dream of trans-forming Irish dancing from the rigid upper torso to the freedom of the Irish spirit using upper body move-ments, Marie's belief in me and my vision made the world open its eyes to this fascinating art form.

Marie's acute attention to detail makes this book the definitive source of information on all things Irish dance and will guide its readers every step of the way!

She is a dear friend, a true blue, and the Queen of Irish Dancing!

Michael Flatley.

Michael Flatley

DEDICATION

To all my Irish dancing friends worldwide.

ACKNOWLEDGEMENTS

Throughout my life I have been privileged to know fantastic people who have been there for me through the good and in particular the bad times. It is not possible to mention everyone by name, but I know that *you* know who you are, and you will be forever in my heart.

I am fortunate to have been a part of many families throughout my life. I was brought up in a great paternal family with a lovely gang of brothers, and a mother and father who had big dreams for me, and sacrificed a great deal to help me make them happen.

I will always be indebted to the Maoileidigh family, and the teachers, dancers and parents at the Inis Ealga Dance School in Dublin where I started my Irish dancing teaching education.

Also, my thanks to all those who helped me establish The Marie Duffy Dance School, to all the dancers who attended classes, and to those who went on to win championships all over the world. Also to my friends from the Irish dancing world in Dublin who supported me throughout this period, in particular Brendan O'Brien, Eugene Harnett and

Isabella Fogarty, and all the colleagues with whom I worked in CLRG over fifty years.

Sincere thanks to the Board of Management of CLRG for allowing me to use extracts from many of their articles and publications to assist with the compilation of this guide. Also to Dr John Cullinane and Orfhlaith Ni Bhriain, both renowned authors and members of An Coimisiun, for their contributions on Irish dance history, the Gaelic League, Irish vocabulary and set dances.

I have had a fabulous, fulfilling life through Irish dancing, culminating in working for one of the best Irish dance shows in the world: 'Lord of the Dance'. I will never forget the opportunity Michael Flatley gave me to join the show, and am profoundly grateful to Michael and Niamh for their close and continuing friendship over the last twenty-five years. Also a big thank-you to all the cast members, musicians and production staff whom I met and worked with during my time with Lord of the Dance. We had a great adventure all over the world, with an abundance of excitement, dramas, laughs and tears. Special thanks to Bernadette Flynn, Damien O'Kane,

Tom Cunningham, James Keegan, Aisling Murphy, and all the other leads and dance captains I had the pleasure to work with.

I am hugely indebted to my very close friends Hilary Joyce Owens and Barry Owens for all their help, advice, monitoring, proof reading and contributions on music and dance over the last eighteen months. Also to their daughter Ella Owens, a fantastic dance pupil and talented model, who kindly agreed to help us with most of the photographs for the guide, taken by our professional photographer, Grant Parfery from Glasgow.

In addition, thanks to Greg at GS Photos in Gerrards Cross for his help in scanning many of the photographs used in the guide.

I am also deeply grateful for the assistance provided by the teaching staff and dance pupils of Scoil Rince Ceim Óir, for many of the photographs, particularly those used in the chapter on céili dancing. Similarly, my thanks to Fernanda Faez, from Brazil, studying for a MA at the University of Limerick, for her photographs, and her insights into the choreographic work combining Irish and Brazilian dance.

It is impossible to mention everybody who has helped me over the years, but specifically I wish to thank my good friend James McCutcheon for all his diligent work as Chairman of the Marie Duffy Foundation, and the tireless efforts he has made to contribute to its success. Also many thanks to Michael O'Doherty, Mary Kerin, Peter O'Grady, Bernadette Flynn, James Moran and Sean Hennigan for their help and contributions to Chapter 9, Health and Safety for Irish Dance Schools.

Thank you to Mona Lennon, John Carey, The Academy Boys and Paula's Wigs and Blings for the use of their photographs in the céilí dancing and headwear sections of the guide.

Finally an enormous thank-you to Mike Pask, my husband, without whose vision, help, encouragement, tenacity and hard work this guide would never have been completed.

Marie, Hilary and Team Céim Óir celebrating at the Worlds in Glasgow 2016.

Marie Duffy Pask at home.

PREFACE

Marie is one of the best choreographers in the world. She is like my twin sister. I will love her forever.

Michael Flatley

I was born on the Cashel Road, Crumlin, Dublin, in 1945, a daughter in a family of seven brothers. My dancing career began at the age of six with dance teacher Maitiu O'Maoileidigh at the world-famous Inis Ealga Dance School in Dublin. By the age of thirteen I had started to create steps for the dance class. Having passed the TCRG exam at the age of twenty, I continued as co-director and teacher at Inis Ealga alongside Maitiu. During this time the school enjoyed success in every category, in every age, and in both the male and female sections at the All Ireland and World Championships, winning over 400 titles in total. The school also won the gold medal for Ireland at the Folk-Dance Olympics in Dijon in 1981. In 1988 I decided to set up the Marie Duffy Irish Dance School in Dublin, which enjoyed continuing success throughout the world and particularly at all 'Majors' – the highest level in competitive dancing.

My dance show career began in 1996 when I was invited by Michael Flatley to work on Lord of the Dance as Dance Director and Associate Choreography. This was followed by Feet of Flames (1999) and Celtic Tiger (2007). I was also involved with the production of all the Lord of the Dance and Celtic Tiger videos. I have travelled all over the world with Michael's shows, touring Taiwan in 2009 with Feet of Flames, and around Europe in 2010 with The Return of Michael Flatley Tour.

Marie Duffy Pask relaxing.

Throughout this period I also worked on many prestigious events including The Prince's Trust and the Ryder Cup in the UK; the Oscars in Los Angeles; Prince Albert's Red Cross Ball in Monaco; and more recently for HRH Prince Charles at Buckingham Palace. Television shows include *Dancing with the Stars* and *Superstars of Dance* in the USA; and *Tonight's the Night*, *Strictly Come Dancing* and

Lord of the Dance cast performing on a European tour.

Marie's CLRG Lifetime Achievement Award with Sean McDonagh and Éilis Uí Dhálaigh (née Nic Shim).

Britain's Got Talent in the UK; as well as Irish dance and music shows, including Irish television's *Beirt Eile* and *Club Ceile*.

As an adjudicator and examiner for CLRG I have judged and examined competitions and exams all over the world, and have been an external examiner for the graduate and masters' courses for Irish Music and Dance at the University of Limerick. I have served on CLRG continuously since 1969, and on many occasions have been the Vice President for England. At the 2011 World Championships, held in my home town of Dublin, I was presented with the first ever Lifetime Achievement Award, which recognized my dedication and contributions to the world of Irish dance and culture.

Later that year, I and my husband set up the Marie Duffy Foundation, a charity formed to help the Irish dancing community. The MDF is a not-for-profit organization to help young dancers follow their dreams and achieve their full potential in Irish dance. The Foundation offers grants to encourage and stimulate creativity, flair and entrepreneurship in the promotion of Irish dance skills and performance.

In March 2015 I retired from Lord of the Dance after twenty years of unbroken service and returned to my first love: teaching Irish dance to the next generation of dancers. I joined Hilary Joyce Owens and her dance school, Scoil Rince Ceim Óir, based just outside the west of London as a dance teacher. Later in 2015, partnering with Eddie Rowley, I wrote my autobiography, *Lady of the Dance*, which was published in March 2017. However, my story has not ended yet – as is the motto of our Foundation:

We go onwards and upwards, improving all the time!

Ar aghaidh linn í bhfeabhas

A Marie Duffy Foundation flysheet.

An innovative modern interpretation of an Irish dance movement in 2021.

INTRODUCTION

Consciousness expresses itself through creation. This world we live in is the dance of the creator. Dancers come and go in the twinkling of an eye but the dance lives on. On many an occasion when I am dancing, I have felt touched by something sacred. In those moments I felt my spirit soar and become one with everything that exists.

Michael Jackson

BACKGROUND

Ireland is known throughout the world for its dancing. The Irish dancing genre is a very important part of the heritage and culture of Ireland together with traditional Irish music, Irish language and Gaelic sports such as hurling and Gaelic football.

Whilst the origins of Irish dancing are uncertain, it is likely that it originated with the Celts and Druids who roamed the Irish countryside before the advent of Christianity.[1] Over the centuries dancing progressively evolved to the form it takes today. Although originally it was a social pastime, in recent times, and particularly over the last 100 years, it has evolved into a global dance form and is actively performed in over thirty countries in five continents. The nature of Irish dance has therefore developed and adapted over recent years to accommodate and reflect changing attitudes and the demands of this wider audience and participants. Nevertheless, it still retains many of the traditional ethical values and dance steps practised in the early days. The control and regulation of worldwide dance schools and competitive events are still based in Ireland,

thus ensuring that in the future Irish dancing will continue to be centred in Ireland.

The teaching of Irish dancing is an increasing and regular extra-curricular activity in numerous Irish schools, and is a practice that has expanded into the UK and beyond. The early introduction of dance lessons at infant and junior level has provided a continuous supply of youngsters to the specialist professional Irish dance schools that have grown worldwide in the last thirty years. In recent years the phenomenal growth and globalization of the art form has also been inspired by the world-wide television exposure of Irish dancing at the Eurovision Song Contest, held in Ireland in 1994. This growth has been further fuelled by the subsequent, universally popular, successful dance shows that have been initiated in recent years.

CONTENT

This guide has been formulated to appeal to all members of the Irish dancing community. It offers a basic introduction for newcomers and novices, and also provides comprehensive and practical instruction for existing Irish dancers, at all levels, from beginners to top level championship dancers. It will provide an invaluable reference manual for Irish dance teachers, dance schools and dance and choreography students. At the same time it is hoped that it will be of great interest to all parents, Irish dance fans and enthusiasts all over the world. It therefore offers a dialogue that encompasses all aspects of the art of Irish dancing from its early beginnings to the modern day, and describes how it has developed globally whilst maintaining the core elements of Irish language, music and culture.

Our story starts with the early beginnings and history of Irish dance and music, dating as far back as the 1600s, and then summarizes the most significant developments since those days to modern times. The changes and advances in dance music, dances and dancing are discussed. In addition, the changing role of the dance master and the evolution of teaching methods are highlighted, together with the influence of innovative musicians and bands and the development of musical instruments. Other major changes in costumes and new fashions to the present day are also outlined.

Moving on, we pose and answer the basic question 'How do I become an Irish dancer?'.

First, the answer to this is dance schools – what they do, and why, where they are, and what is involved.

The key dance steps and formations are discussed in detail, and the main elements of solo dancing, céilí dancing, figure choreography and show dancing are featured. The importance and basics of Irish dance are examined, such as posture, use of the arms, time and rhythm. As with most dance genres, a unique language is used in Irish dancing, and a list and explanation of the most commonly used words and phrases is included. Newcomers to Irish dancing are always keenly interested in the dance wear worn – what it is and when it is worn. The following main fashion items are therefore covered:

Shoes: A description of the types of shoe commonly used for different dance – where to get them, and typical costs.
Dresses: The types of dress commonly used for different dance forms – where to get them and typical costs, from simple tunics to championship dresses.
Headwear: The various types of wig and alternatives – when to wear them and where to buy them, and typical costs.
Make-up: Advice on the best techniques, and how to use make-up to enhance your appearance and appeal.

Musicality in Irish dance is explored, together with an explanation of the critical music terms as they relate to Irish dancing. The music is an integral part of Irish dancing, and a unique library of scores has evolved over the years – the one doesn't exist without the other! It is essential that the Irish dancer has an appreciation and understanding of how important the music is, and how the various tunes relate to the dance.

The aspiring dancer is guided through all the key elements involved in the specific dance steps, music formations and patterns that feature in solo dancing, céilí dancing and figure choreography at all levels. These are presented in an easily understandable way with the aid of sketches and photographs.

Modern Irish dancing is highly professional, and a section is therefore included on teacher and adjudicator qualifications – what they are, what you need to know, how to apply to get them, and most importantly how to be successful. The guide then explores the worlds of competitive and show dancing, with many practical tips and a great deal of advice on how to succeed in these fields. A range of other educational and career opportunities potentially open to Irish dancers is identified for those wishing to remain in Irish dancing when their competitive careers are over.

Irish dancing is part of our heritage and culture, but it has become a very athletic pastime, and in conjunction with some notable contributors, the importance of factors such as diet, training,

A typical modern Irish dance school in action in 2021.

preparation, mindset and how to succeed is discussed. 'Best practice' in these essential areas is defined. The guide also provides a comprehensive reference manual for dance schools and dance teachers in the management and running of their schools, particularly with respect to child protection and health and safety matters.

HOW TO USE THIS GUIDE

I truly hope that *The Essential Guide to Irish Dance* will become the instructional bible for all those involved in Irish dancing at all levels. To the newcomer it can be used as a road map into dance to help them become an enthusiastic social dancer, or as a comprehensive manual to establish a professional career in the world of dance. To the championship dancer it can be used to develop a greater understanding of the intricacies of advanced steps, to help them appreciate the artistic qualities necessary to prepare exciting set dances, and above all show them how to choreograph that exclusive and innovative piece of Irish dance.

To the dance teacher and dance school it can be used as a textbook on all aspects of Irish dancing, from the first steps, through céilí dancing, and to the ultimate challenge of choreographing innovative figure dances and dance dramas for world championships. In addition it will provide schools with the detail and procedures necessary to obtain formal dance qualifications. Finally, the reader will find invaluable advice and programmes on other crucial aspects such as musicality, and the influence of body and mind, all of which will enable dancers to achieve their full potential and fulfil their dreams in the world of Irish dance.

An early shot of Irish dancing at a crossroads on the outskirts of an Irish village.

CHAPTER 1

THE HISTORY AND DEVELOPMENT OF IRISH DANCE

Dance is the timeless interpretation of life.
Through synergy of intellect, artistry and grace
came into existence the blessing of a dancer.
Shah Asad Rizvi

HISTORY

Opinion is divided as to the exact origins of Irish dance. However, what is certain is that it has been around in some form for centuries, although its earliest form would be far removed from modern-day Irish dance. I have researched the history of Irish dance for this guide, and have pieced together extracts from a number of sources to provide a possible picture of the evolution of the dance form to what it is today.

The Early Records

But when and how did it all start? It is likely that the early history of Irish dance grew from a variety of factors, such as migration, wars and invasions over the centuries, resulting in a significant change in the population demographics. The arrival of these foreign nationalities introduced a variety of new cultures, including dance and music, that were ultimately to herald the birth of Irish dancing in its earliest form. Clearly the history of Irish dance is interwoven with the overall history of Ireland itself,

and it is likely that influences resulted from the four most recent civilizations prevalent in Ireland, namely the Druids, the Celts, the Vikings and the Anglo-Normans.

There are only vague references to the early history of Irish dancing. For example, there is some, albeit sketchy, evidence of the Druids dancing in religious ceremonies in which they worshipped a number of idols such as oak trees and the sun. In addition there is evidence that extracts from some of their circular dances survive in the ring dances of today.[2] So maybe this can be considered as the start of dance in Ireland.

It is generally accepted that the Celts arrived in Ireland around two thousand years ago, bringing with them their own folk dances and music – another possible influence on dancing in Ireland. Then in about the fifth century, in spite of the conversion to Christianity in Ireland, the indigenous peasants continued to retain the same qualities in their music and dancing.

The Vikings first invaded Ireland in AD795, when a small group of Norse warriors attacked a monastery on the east coast. They plundered the monastery of its valuables, such as relics, and laid them to waste. The history of the Vikings in Ireland spans over 200 years, and although it can be considered shortlived, the Viking invaders did make important

OPPOSITE: **Lord of the Dance performing to an excited audience during the return of a Michael Flatley tour.**

contributions to the Irish way of life: they settled, intermarried, and shared their culture with the Irish, and this almost certainly included music and dance.

Following the collapse of the Viking era, the Anglo-Norman conquest of Ireland began with the Anglo-Norman invasion in 1169, and this brought Norman customs and culture to Ireland. These included the Norman dance known as 'the Carol': this combined singing and dancing and featured a circle of dancers, and was regularly performed in Irish towns.[2]

The 'Ireland's Eye'[2] identifies a number of possible forerunners to today's dances. Three Irish dances often mentioned in sixteenth-century articles were notably the Irish Hey, the Rince Fada and the Trenchmore (*see below*). An early reference to dance is contained in a letter written by Sir Henry Sydney to Queen Elizabeth I in 1569, which spoke about magnificently dressed and first-class dancers performing enthusiastic Irish jigs in Galway. He reported that the dancers were in two straight lines, which perhaps suggests they were performing an early version of the long dance.

During the mid-sixteenth century dancing was becoming increasingly popular, with regular performances in the newly built castles and stately homes. The Hey was very popular at the time, and involved the female dancers winding in around their partners – an early version of the modern-day reel. Another popular dance was the Trenchmore, which was adapted by the 'English Invaders' from an old Irish peasant dance. It was common that when royalty arrived in Ireland, they were met by women performing local dances. Typically, three people, holding the ends of a white handkerchief, stood abreast: then advancing to slow music, they were followed by dancing couples. The tempo of the music then increased, allowing the dancers to break out into a range of other dance formations.[2] Dancing was also regularly performed at wakes, held to remember and celebrate the life of a departed soul. The mourners followed each other in a ring round the coffin, dancing to the bagpipe music popular at the time.

There is also some documentary evidence that dancing was widespread throughout rural Ireland at the start of the seventeenth century. It is at this time that the Irish word for dance emerged: 'rince'. An earlier report also mentioned that Irish dances closely resembled English country dances, further confirming the early English influence on the development of Irish dance. The distinctive hornpipe rhythm of the Irish dance tradition had developed by the 1760s, and with the arrival of the fiddle from the European continent, a new class of dance master began to emerge.

The development of traditional Irish dancing steps and formations almost certainly grew in association with the trends in Irish music. The features commonly associated with Irish dance were born at this time: the local dancing venues were usually small, and often dances were demonstrated on table tops, where space for expansive movement was inevitably restricted. Consequently it was necessary to hold the arms rigidly at each side of the body, given the lack of space for lateral movement. This is possibly one of several credible explanations for this highly visible characteristic of Irish dancers. In time, larger dance venues became available, and so there was greater opportunity to include more movement in and round the dance area.

The Irish Dance Master

You dance love, and you dance joy, and you dance dreams. And I know if I can make you smile by jumping over a couple of couches or running through a rainstorm, then I'll be very glad to be your song and dance man.

Gene Kelly

As mentioned earlier, the advent of the dance master occurred around the end of the 1700s, and travelling dance masters regularly taught across rural Ireland as late as the eighteenth and early nineteenth centuries. 'Ireland's Eye' highlights the role and importance of the dance master. He was a wandering dancing teacher who travelled, within an area, around the many villages teaching dance to peasants. They were flamboyant characters who wore bright clothes and carried staffs.[2]

Group dances of a very high standard were developed by the masters to hold the interest of their less gifted pupils and to give them the chance to enjoy dancing. Solo dancers were held in high esteem, and often doors were taken off their hinges and placed on the ground for the soloists to dance on. Every dance master had his own district and never encroached on another's territory. However, it was not unknown for a dance master to be kidnapped by the residents of a neighbouring parish. When dance masters met at fairs, they challenged each other to a public dancing contest that only ended when one of them dropped with fatigue. Several versions of the same dance were to be found in different parts of Ireland. In this way a rich heritage of Irish dances was assembled and modified over the centuries.

Today, jigs, reels, hornpipes, sets, half sets and step dances are all performed.[2]

Early Costumes

Irish dancing dresses have changed dramatically over the years. Dancers in the eighteenth and nineteenth centuries wore their 'Sunday best', simply wearing the outfit that they normally wore to church. Typically, early costumes were made of hand-woven tweed fabrics. The costumes were loosely based on the leine (tunic) and the brat (stole or cape), as depicted in images from eighth-century illuminated Irish manuscripts.[1]

Dancers started to develop more formal dance wear from around the early 1900s. In the mid nineteen-fifties dresses were based on the Irish peasant dress worn two hundred years ago. Most of the dresses were adorned with hand-embroidered Celtic designs and copies of the Tara brooch were

Dance costume of the 1950s showing a cape and Tara brooches. Marie's first dance costume!

Development of women's and men's costumes in the 1960s: longer sleeves, Irish wool dresses and more Celtic designs for the women's dresses, and Irish tweed jackets and wool socks for the men.

often worn on the shoulder. The brooch held a cape that fell over the back.

Each school of dancing has its own distinct dancing costume. From the 1940s onwards one of the ways in which dance schools defined themselves was through the wearing of class costumes wlth specific colours and embroidcry motifs. These simple knee-length dresses with

Major changes to dresses in the early 1980s with the use of velvet for dresses, deep Irish lace crochet collars, and more elaborate Celtic embroidery.

World céilí champions in the 1990s: the Marie Duffy School.

World-class style of costume from the early 1980s.

World-class style of costume from the early 1990s.

World-class style of costume from the late 1980s.

World-class style of costume from the late 1990s.

long sleeves and full skirts had embroidery on the skirt, bodice and cape, with crochet lace collar and cuffs worked in cotton. For male dancers it was common to wear a kilt, with shirt and tie, under a wool blazer.[1]

In the 1970s and 1980s solo dancers began to wear heavy A-line dresses embroidered with a variety of Celtic patterns. The dancing dresses of today are designed to the dancers' individual taste, and each one is unique. Different colours, patterns and materials ensure that each solo dancer stands out from the crowd. Apart from dresses, wigs are also worn by dancers, and fake tan, make up and tiaras are also commonplace. This is vastly different from the early 1900s when the Gaelic League (Conradh na Gaeilge) was formed to promote Irish culture and heritage:[3] then the design of the dresses was based on the style of dress worn by Irish peasants. However, the Irish dancing industry has moved with the times, and large competitions (feiseanna) are held in huge arenas and theatres complete with proper stages and lighting.

Originally, the dresses worn by women were copies of the traditional Irish peasant dress; they were adorned with hand-embroidered Celtic designs based on the *Book of Kells* and Irish stone crosses. The dancers of today who compete at country and world level need to stand out from the crowd with their flamboyant dresses, fake tan, make-up and tiaras! The material has changed from Irish wool to velvet and the lightweight materials of today. Embroidery has gone out of fashion, and the addition of plenty of sparkles and 'diamonds' is far more popular today.

There are two types of costume traditionally worn by boys who compete in Irish dancing competitions: a kilt or long black trousers. Kilts have been worn for many years, but nowadays the dancers prefer to wear long black trousers when competing, with an embroidered waistcoat or jacket.

As you can see from the photographs, today's dresses have changed dramatically from those worn in the early years. The success of the World

Championships over the last fifty years has fuelled a revolution in costume design for both females and males. The popularity of curly wigs and elaborate dresses shows no signs of diminishing, and has led to a growth industry for commercially produced Feis costumes. For grade competitions the costumes are simpler and more traditional in style.[1]

Irish Dance Music

Irish dance and the music of Ireland have been inextricably linked over centuries. An assortment of instruments has provided the music for dancing throughout this period, and these are discussed in more detail in Chapter 3.

Historically the traditional accompaniment for Irish dancing was a harp and bagpipes, or just singing, known as *port a beil*. However, as the dances became more complex, so did the music, and there is a now a wider variety of music and instruments to accompany the music. Some typical Irish instruments include the fiddle, the bodhran (a handheld drum), the tin whistle, the concertina, the button and piano accordions, and the uilleann pipes.[4]

In the seventeenth century bagpipers and harpers were the principal musicians – but when they were prevented from playing in public by legislation, an assortment of other musicians provided the beat. Many of these musicians were blind or had other physical disabilities, and music offered them a reasonable regular income. In later years the harpers teamed up with the dance masters for their regular visits and dance classes.

From the end of the eighteenth century dancing at wakes was another familiar sight. The mourners would follow each other in a ring round the coffin to the music of the bagpipes. When no instrument was available the lilter provided the music. Lilting, or *port a beil*, is a unique musical sound produced with the mouth.[5] The music was never written down, and musicians played and learned tunes by ear. Their tunes were passed from one generation to the next. They must have had excellent memories as a skilled

World-class style of costume from the 2020s.

musician could play any one of several hundred tunes on request.[5]

The majority of Irish jigs are native in origin and were composed by pipers and fiddlers in conjunction with the dance master. In addition, some of the tunes were rearrangements of English or Scottish tunes, for example the 'Fairy Reel', which was composed in Scotland in 1802, became popular in Ireland a century later. Often, many dance tune titles had no musical connection with the actual tunes – the musician often looked around his immediate environment for inspiration when naming a composition.

Music at céilíthe today is provided by a céilí band, with musicians playing an assortment of instruments including the fiddle, drums, piano and accordion.[5] Live music is always employed at registered feiseanna (dance competitions), usually with one or two accomplished musicians playing the music.

Formation of the Gaelic League

In 1893 the Gaelic League (Conradh na Gaeilge) was founded as an organization to promote and encourage all aspects of Irish culture in Ireland. The primary purpose was to promote a national pride in Irish language, literature, music, song, dance and sports.[3] Although the promotion of dance and music was not the primary object of the League, it was at that time that dancing was referred to as Irish dancing and the dances were termed the national dances of Ireland.[6]

Prior to the Gaelic League, formal dance classes were centred round rural areas such as Cork, Kerry and Limerick. The League spawned a desire for more Irish dancing, for entertainment, exhibition and competition. It organized formal competitions, lessons and rules. This resulted in an increased demand for more and regular dance classes, including a geographic expansion into places such as Dublin and London. More often than not dance classes were held in conjunction with Irish language classes, particularly outside the traditional Irish centres. As the League grew in popularity in the dance world it introduced regular weekly dance classes; dance competitions called feiseanna; regional, national and international championships called oireachtaisi; and special costumes and céilí dances for both social and competitive occasions.[6]

The League's interest in and guidance for the control of Irish dancing continued from its inception in 1893 through to the 1930s. However, in the late 1920s behaviour at feiseanna deteriorated, and the local dancing teachers' associations appeared to be unable to control this. Accordingly, the League became even more involved in the administration of Irish dancing, and after a series of initiatives, finally set up Coimisiún an Rinnce (the Dancing Commission) on 8 March 1930. Ultimately responsible to the Gaelic League, this commission was responsible for the administration of Irish dancing, both solo and figure dancing, throughout Ireland. The title remained unchanged until 1943 when it was modified to An Coimisiún le Rincí Galelacha (CLRG), a title it has retained to this day.[6]

THE GROWTH OF IRISH DANCING GLOBALLY

The world-wide success of Riverdance and Lord of the Dance has placed Irish dance on the international stage. Today, dance schools worldwide are filled with young pupils keen to imitate and learn the dancing styles that brought Jean Butler and Michael Flatley international acclaim. Today there are many opportunities to watch, enjoy and practise Irish dancing. It is still a regular part of social functions. Dancing sessions at céilíthe are usually preceded by a teaching period where novices are shown the initial steps. During the summer months, céilíthe are held in many Irish towns. Visitors are always welcome to join in, and with on-the-spot, informal instruction, anyone can quickly master the first steps and soon share the Irish enthusiasm for Irish dance.[2]

The growth of Irish dancing since the formation of CLRG has been phenomenal. Initially very much Irish, and to a smaller extent British based, the organization became an international body in the 1960s and 1970s when it registered its first teachers from America, Canada, Australia and New Zealand. Examinations in both Ireland and the New World countries significantly increased in this period as international travel became cheaper and more readily available. The number of dance schools registered with CLRG also dramatically increased, usually in traditionally Irish-based communities, and as a result there were significant increases in dancer numbers. This growing globalization led to the first Irish Dancing World Championships in 1970.

This further fuelled the huge increases in the number of schools and dancers, as the international appeal of a truly top-class competition generated huge interest. The first World Championships, held in Dublin, attracted entries from the USA, Canada, England, Scotland and Ireland. This prestigious annual event was scheduled to celebrate its fiftieth anniversary in Dublin in April 2020, but unfortunately was cancelled due to the Covid 19 pandemic. By this time the international appeal and interest in Irish dancing had grown to such an extent that competitors from no fewer than thirty countries were registered for the event. Thankfully the event took place in Belfast in April 2022.

New Irish dancing schools and dancers have sprung up in east and west Europe, Russia, China, Taiwan, South Africa, Mexico and Latin America in the last ten years. There are currently over 2,300 Irish dance teachers registered with CLRG, and an estimated 500 dance schools world-wide. Over 5,000 competitors were expected to compete at the 2020 World Championships, attracting an estimated audience of around 40,000.

Mixed céilí team costume style in the early 1960s.

Present-day ladies' team costume style.

The Role and Growth of Competitive Dancing

The Irish word céilí originally referred to a gathering of neighbours in a house intent on having an enjoyable time, dancing, playing music, singing and storytelling. Today it mainly refers to an informal evening of dancing. Céilíthe are held in large towns and country districts where young and old enjoy group dances together. The céilí can be traced back to pre-famine times, when dancing at the cross-roads was a popular rural pastime.

These dances were usually held on Sunday evenings in the summer when young people would gather at the cross-roads. The music was often performed by a fiddler seated on a three-legged stool with his upturned hat beside him for a collection. The fiddler began with a reel such as the lively 'Silver Tip', but he had to play it several times before the dancers joined in. The young men would be reluctant to begin the dance, but after some encouragement from the fiddler, the sets of eight filled up the dancing area.[2]

The first form of competitive dancing probably evolved from these local céilíthe. Inevitably, as the numbers grew a desire for competition evolved, resulting in the introduction of the ever-popular feis, where dancers of all ages competed in separate competitions for feis titles. The feis has been an important part of rural cultural life with children, teenagers and adults competing in separate competitions for the feis titles and prizes. There are both group (céilí) and solo (step dancing) competitions, where dancers are graded by age from five to seventeen and then into the senior categories.[2]

Following the formation of CLRG, the regulatory body started to codify and standardize step-dancing competition and education. Over subsequent decades as CLRG expanded globally it promoted this form of step dancing by introducing examinations and qualifications for teachers and competition adjudicators. Today, for most competing countries there are several levels of competition divided by age, gender, ability and location, ranging from county to regional and national competitions.[1]

Show Dancing

It was back in 1994 that Michael Flatley and Jean Butler burst on to the scene with a seven-minute routine known as Riverdance, which took place during the interval of the 1994 Eurovision Song Contest held in Ireland. This feature presented Irish dancing in a different form to a world-wide

Typical modern dance show ensemble.

audience, and generated a new, enthusiastic group of fans and dancers.

The other main factor driving the increased interest in and popularity of Irish dancing has been the advent of stage shows such as Riverdance and Lord of the Dance, which followed the highly successful Eurovision Spectacular. The nature of the Irish dance tradition has changed and adapted over the years to accommodate and reflect changing populations and the fusion of new cultures. The popular new shows have reinvigorated Irish dancing.[3]

Flying high from Celtic Tiger – showcasing the choreographic, set and costume developments of show dancing.

The glamour and acrobatics of show dancing.

The initial dance shows have been running uninterrupted for over twenty-five years and have wowed audiences all over the world. Other innovative shows have also been highly successful, and new choreography is being developed all the time. Of particular interest is the fusion of Irish dance with other dance genres.

Overall I believe that the long-term future for all aspects of Irish dancing is positive and rosy, and it will continue to prosper and grow both in the traditional heartlands of Ireland but also in an increasing number of nations worldwide. The future is indeed green, white and orange.

The Irish colours.

CHAPTER 2

HOW DO I BECOME AN IRISH DANCER?

The job of feet is walking but their hobby is dancing.

Amit Kalantri

HOW DO I START?

There are two primary routes into Irish dancing: first via professional tuition in an accredited Irish dance school; or by teaching yourself via instruction manuals and on-line tuition courses. Both routes have advantages and disadvantages, and the first step is to identify which route is the best for you. This will depend very much upon individual circumstances, such as where you live, your financial position, and above all your ultimate goal in Irish dancing. In the next few paragraphs there will be guidance on some of the main factors that you may wish to consider in deciding which might be the most appropriate route for you.

Professional Tuition in an Irish Dance School

There are many hundreds of Irish dance schools throughout the world, but where are they, what do they do, and how do you select the right school for you?

Finding Your Potential Dance School

There are four main sources of information:

- Your friends and neighbours – often a good choice, as personal experience and recommendation is often the best choice.

- Your local press and community organizations such as the Citizens Advice Bureau – can be very useful for identifying if, and where, there are any suitable schools in your local area.
- International dance organizations – the main ones are listed later and described in this chapter. These will provide comprehensive lists of schools operating worldwide, together with their endorsement and accreditation where appropriate.
- Your own on-line enquiries through the major search engines such as Google, Safari.

Opportunities and Advantages

So what opportunities and advantages can I expect to receive by joining a dance school? As with most organizations in life, dance schools come in many forms and sizes, and it is important that you choose a school that most meets your goals, aspirations and preferences. Most schools teach both solo and céilí dancing, but often specialize in one form or the other. Again, most schools have a range of classes to suit various levels of experience and competency, from beginners to championship level and at the intermediate levels in between. Classes usually last from between two and three hours, and can consist of individual or group sessions. The larger and better schools have programmes that will specifically train dancers to achieve and obtain the grade qualifications discussed in Chapter 6.

Choosing a Dance School

So, what factors should I consider when choosing my dance school? Listed below are a number of

A dance school in action.

some of the key factors to take into account when making your decision. This list is not exhaustive, and there may well be others that are particularly relevant to you.

- The size and number of pupils in the school is important – do you want to join a large, top-class school, or would you feel more comfortable in a smaller and perhaps more sociable one?
- Its location will be crucial – travelling long distances can be very time consuming, costly and tiring – especially if you decide to attend two, three or multiple classes a week.
- What is the school's prospectus, including its teaching programme of classes, times and costs, and will they meet your requirements?
- What is the school's ethos – does it have a mission statement, objects, and a three-year business plan?
- What facilities does it have – does the school own or rent its own studio and use dancing facilities such as mirrors, bars, modern sound systems and video recording equipment?
- What is its track record in terms of dancing examination success and pass rates?
- Does it have any champion dancers, or do you just want to join a social class?
- How many teachers does the school employ, and what are their qualifications and experience?

An exercise and balance bar – an essential dance teaching tool.

- Are *all* the teachers vetted and cleared to teach children, and have they passed all the necessary vetting procedures?

Once you have all the data and answers you will be in a position to evaluate your options, select your school, and start on your dancing journey.

Self-Teaching with Media and On-Line Support
The simplest way to start building a knowledge of, and practice in Irish dancing is to choose the self-teaching route. There are numerous opportunities available for the beginner to start to learn the basic steps and formations in Irish dancing, including of course this guide.

Self-Teaching
Self-teaching is probably the cheapest way to start to learn the basics of Irish dancing. However, it has major limitations once the basics have been learnt, and if you wish to progress into competitive dancing. Nevertheless, for many it is possibly the only way to get started because of financial limitations, travel restrictions and/or the availability of a suitable dance school. If you select this route, it is important that you do this within a structured learning regime with a programme and a plan.[7] The key elements of this would include the following:

- What is your ultimate goal – how far do you wish to go, and will your proposed plan meet your objective?
- Management of your time – for how long, and when will you be self-learning?
- Setting up learning objectives and milestones.
- Identification and purchase of your training material and reference points – books, manuals, videos and so on.
- Identification and procurement of the facilities and equipment you will need, such as computers, music players, office space, dance space, flooring, dance wear and so on.
- How will you evaluate your learning progress and competency?
- Thoughts as to how you can partner up with other dancers, mentors and teachers.

The main advantages of the self-learning approach are:

- Cost – it is cheaper than going to, and paying for a dance class, and the travel costs are minimal.
- Potentially more efficient, since all the learning process is focused on you.
- It enables individual control of the scope and time of your learning programme.

The main disadvantages are:

- The lack of a professionally qualified instructor.
- The lack of other students with whom to interreact and share ideas.
- It must be totally self-motivating.
- There is limited instructional material beyond the beginner and basics levels.

Books and Instruction Manuals
There are several publications that provide a very good starting point for the beginner, including of course this guide, and these can be found both on-line, or purchased from the major book shops. The publications tend to be very good at describing basic techniques and movements, and are particularly useful when used in conjunction with the moving images in a DVD or video.

DVDs and Videos
Again, there are numerous products available that can provide instructive and practical help through visual moving images. It is always advisable to use products and recordings that have been prepared and produced by a fully qualified dance teacher. It is particularly important that you use professionally trained people when using exercising and/or physical training routines.

Social Media
In recent years there has been a massive increase in the use of media outlets such as YouTube, Twitter, Facebook, TikTok and Instagram as an outlet for displaying and exploring many aspects of Irish dance steps. This is particularly true of the top dancers, who increasingly use these platforms for sharing their undoubted talent and choreography expertise. These will be extremely valuable for more advanced dancers who are keen to experiment with

innovative steps and to develop their own choreographical talents.

IRISH DANCE ORGANIZATIONS

Global Irish dancing is administered and governed by a number of organizations. The primary roles of these bodies are typically as follows:

- To set and administer the general rules of both solo, céilí dancing and figure dancing.
- To register and certify dance schools and dance teachers.
- To set qualifications and syllabi for dancer and teacher examinations.
- To organize examinations.
- To administer all aspects of procedures and rules for authorized feiseanna.

They are also an extremely good source of information regarding all aspects of Irish dancing, particularly for details of dancing and teacher qualifications; examination venues and dates; dance schools; locations and dates for feiseanna. Contact details for all the major bodies are given in the references at the end of the book.

The following organizations are currently operating globally, together with some information about their origins, aims and programmes obtained from their individual websites. Whilst they all have similar goals and aspirations, they do have different priorities and specialities.

An Coimisiún le Rincí Gaelacha (CLRG) – The Irish Dancing Commission

This is the largest governing body with its head office and full-time staff located in Dublin. It is the oldest organization controlling Irish dance, formed in 1929 operating under the auspices of the Gaelic League. Initially a commission of enquiry into how dance events in Ireland were organized, its function was then changed to include responsibility for the organization and running of all dance competitions. Since then it has grown enormously, and it administers at least 2,000 registered dance schoolteachers, with an estimated number of dancers of over 60,000.

The objective of An Coimisiún is to preserve and promote Irish dancing, including step dancing, céilí dancing and other team dancing, and also to promote the use of the Irish language and all aspects of Irish culture. Its mission statement is as follows:

The main objective of An Coimisiún le Rincí Gaelacha is the preservation and promotion of Irish dancing, including step dancing, céilí dancing and other team dancing. While of course its main function is the promotion of Irish dance, An Coimisiún is proud of working in association with Conradh na Gaeilge in promoting all aspects of Irish culture, including the use and promotion of the Irish language.

CLRG promotes, and is active in, all aspects of Irish dancing worldwide. It organizes competitions, examinations and seminars.[8]

An Comhdháil na Múinteoirí le Rincí Gaelacha: Congress of Irish Dance Teachers

This congress was formed in 1969, when a number of teachers and adjudicators parted with CLRG and established their own independent organization. Although not well documented, the split was thought to be due to aesthetic and ideological conflicts due to the lack of substantial representation of practising teachers on the Board of An Coimisiún. An Chomhdháil is today the second-largest Irish dance organization, and one of six to run a World Championships competition. An Chomhdháil operates a system of examinations for the registration of teachers and adjudicators, and regulates Irish stepdance at its hierarchical system of competitions held across the world.[9]

Cumann Rince Náisiúnta (CRN): Nation Dance Association

Established in 1982, CRN is now a worldwide organization. With members in Ireland, England, Wales, Holland and the USA, its stated policy is 'to encourage and protect tradition within Irish dancing. In terms of repertoire the preservation of traditional set dances is considered of paramount importance.'

CRN was founded in 1982 by the late Ita Cadwell, along with eleven other teachers. As their website says:

They believed that all teachers should be protected, and that all dancers should be afforded the right to dance.

Since its formation, CRN has encouraged an open platform for all dancers and provides an organization that gives a voice to young teachers. Most importantly it provides a stage where every dancer can perform in a competitive but friendly environment. CRN is governed by an executive committee who are elected by their members to uphold their constitution. Their feiseanna are run under their own rules of competition.[10]

Comhaltas Ceoltóirí Éireann: Gathering of Musicians of Ireland

This organization was founded in Mullingar, Ireland, in 1951 to preserve Irish music, dance, language and other aspects of Irish culture.

Comhaltas Ceoltóirí Éireann is the largest group involved in the preservation and promotion of Irish traditional music. They are a non-profit-making cultural movement with hundreds of local branches around the world, and have been working for the cause of Irish music since the middle of the last century. Their efforts continue with increasing zeal as the movement launches itself into the twenty-first century.

Comhaltas has grown with the times, and today they are proud to be the foremost movement preserving and promoting Irish traditional music. Branches of Comhaltas have formed in every county in Ireland and also abroad, organizing classes, concerts and sessions in local communities with active branches in the United States, Britain, Canada, Japan and elsewhere. In fact there are hundreds of branches in fifteen countries on four continents.[11]

Cumman Rínce Dea Mheasa

Based in Ireland and the United Kingdom, CRDM describes itself as an organization for goodwill and excellence in Irish dancing. Its stated objective is 'to preserve the history and promote the future of Irish dancing as well as the culture, language and music in Ireland.' Its mission statement is 'CRDM is a young dynamic and professional organization whose aim is to unite and support its members, and to promote and preserve Irish dancing.'[12]

DANCE FORMS

Whilst the beginner is primarily concerned with learning the basic steps in Irish dancing, once this is conquered, their aspirations turn to acquiring a greater knowledge of and participation in more complex dance movements.

All forms of traditional Irish dance are identified by the same basic concepts, but there are four main dance forms that are characterized by specific steps, formations and, at the competitive level, rules. These are solo dancing, céilí dancing, figure dancing and dance drama. However, in the last twenty-five years new dance forms have emerged as the truly innovative and creative dancers of the times have moved further away from many of the traditional steps, and have created unique and original new steps and formations. These innovators not only created novel pieces, but also nurtured a new phenomenon at the same time – namely show dancing. In turn this has spawned a flood of other new innovative choreography.

Solo Dancing (Step Dancing)

Probably the most popular and common dance form taught in the majority of dance schools and at all levels of competitive dancing is solo dancing. It is basically split into two main dance types based on the type of shoe worn, namely the soft shoe (a light shoe) or the hard shoe (a heavy shoe). More detail on the shoes themselves is given in the section 'Dance Wear' later in this chapter.

There are four main soft-shoe dance styles: the reel, the slip jig, the light jig and the single jig. Each type is differentiated by different time signatures and with different emphasis within the measure, thus distinguishing the music. Hard-shoe dances include the hornpipe, the heavy jig, the treble reel, traditional sets and open set dances. The open set

A solo dance in action.

A céilí team learning the roly poly from the Three Tunes.

dance differs from the traditional set dance as it is choreographed and very innovative – the speeds also differ. At the competitive level there is also a set dance with a different format to the traditional set dance.

The whole of Chapter 4 is devoted to solo dancing, and the full details of the steps and movements are described there.

Céilí Dancing

Irish céilí dancing is the original community group dance of Ireland and is danced to traditional Irish music throughout the country. Some céilí dances can be traced back to the 1500s, and most are danced to reels or jigs. Céilí dances can have various formations, including two couples (Four Hand Reel and Humours of Bandon), three couples (Duke Reel), four couples (Morris Reel, Eight-Hand Jig), six couples (Lannigan's Ball), or eight couples (Sixteen-Hand Reel) in a group; also lines of two opposite two (Walls of Limerick, Antrim Reel), three opposite three (Fairy Reel, Harvest Time Jig) or four opposite four (Siege of Ennis). Each line would progress to meet a new line of dancers and repeat the same movements with them: these are described as progressive dances.

Some dances are performed by a line of men facing a line of women (Haymakers Jig, Rince Fada), while others are performed by any number of couples in a circle (Rince Mór).

The whole of Chapter 5 is devoted to céilí dancing, and full details of the formations and routines can be found there.

Figure Dancing and Dance Drama

These dance forms are showcased at the larger competitive events, and allow dance schools to use imagination and new choreography outside the strict rules regarding solo or traditional céilí dances. Figure dancing allows for a group choreography for up to sixteen people using common céilí motifs as well as new movements. Dance drama is a competition in which an original written story is told through dance and mime and music. The use of props and original costumes to help the storytelling is encouraged.

Dance drama, Brazilian style.

The pinnacle of creative choreography Irish style.

Generally speaking, figure dances are abstract, whereas the dance drama is a form of narrative dance.

Show Dancing

Irish dance shows come in a variety of forms, varying from the major global touring shows such as Lord of the Dance and Riverdance, to much smaller shows usually based in Ireland and mainly in Dublin. The major shows, usually lasting around two hours, consist of around fifteen to twenty different dance numbers of varying choreography. A typical touring group would employ around forty dancers, with the occasional show involving up to eighty performers. The smaller shows involve fewer dancers and are often shorter in length, and perform in small theatres, hotels or pubs. Needless to say most show dancers, invariably professional, come from the top echelons

The new world – the freedom that Irish show dancing offers for creative choreography.

of competitive dancing and could number a total of around 300 to 500 dancers at any point in time.

Innovative Choreography

An increasing amount of innovative choreography is being developed in today's dancing world. This usually involves small groups, often consisting of a single performer as well as small teams of, say, up to six. These avant-garde choreographers, sometimes in conjunction with university graduates and students, are not only developing Irish dance well beyond its original forms, but are also working with star dancers from other dance genres to create exciting new productions. There are several advanced prestigious workshops, seminars and work camps that the enthusiast can join to explore their own potential and develop new ideas.

THE BASICS OF TRADITIONAL IRISH DANCE

Characterized by a rigid torso and dances performed high on the balls of the feet, this style became popular from the late nineteenth century when the Gaelic League began efforts to preserve and promote Irish dance as part of a broader nationalist movement concerned with Irish culture. Although a rigid torso may be the initial characterization of Irish dance, modern soft-shoe Irish ballerinas commonly use their arms gracefully in flowing movements, abandoning the traditional form. It is not uncommon for hard-shoe dancers to utilize their arms in strict hand formations, other than holding them at their sides.

Detailed information will be given in chapters 4 and 5 on the specific characteristics of each step within an individual dance, but there are a number of specifics general to all traditional Irish dancing, and it is essential that beginners learn these early on and remember them every time they perform.

THE LANGUAGE OF IRISH DANCE

There is a unique language used in Irish dancing, which is even more complicated, as many of the terms and definitions are used in both English and Gaelic languages. One of the best published reference books on the subject is *The Terminology of Irish Dance* by Orfhlaith Ní Bhriain[13] of the University of Limerick, and it is recommended that all dance schools should have a copy of, or access to, this excellent work. It is an invaluable reference work with terms in English and Gaelic covering areas such as dances, dance steps and techniques; social dance; competitive dance and historical contexts. Many of the terms may be used throughout this book so I have included the most commonly used terms, which will not be familiar to a newcomer, in Appendix 2.

THE MUSIC OF IRISH DANCE

Much of what we now call traditional Irish music originated in the Gaelic-speaking peasantry of the eighteenth century, and at the time dancing was a very popular social activity at numerous social events. It was at that time that the dance masters consolidated dances and music into a number of different dance forms depending on the music timings and beats.

The main dance forms and their music used today are as follows:

The jig: The jig is the oldest form of dance. There are three types, which are discussed in detail in Chapter 3. The Lark in the Morning and Morrison's Jig are examples of well-known jigs. Slip jigs include The Butterfly and the opening of Riverdance.

The reel: The reel is of Scottish descent and is often the favourite dance of traditional musicians. Drowsy Maggie, The Mason's Apron, the Wind that Shakes the Barley and Toss the Feathers are examples of well-known reels.

The hornpipe: The hornpipe is the slowest dance, leaving room for the most complicated of dance steps. Many set dances are hornpipes. Other dances related to hornpipes include barn dances, and highlands. The Harvest Home and King of the Fairies are good examples of hornpipes.

DANCE WEAR

One of the first questions a new dancer frequently asks is 'What must I wear?' The public image of an Irish dance costume is of the very expensive ornate and often ostentatious costumes and wigs seen in top competitions and shows, and the dancer may ask: 'Do I need to buy these to start?' The simple answer is 'no'. The cost of competition apparel is very high – a top class competition dress could cost over a thousand pounds. Dance wear for modern traditional and modern Irish dancing at the average dance school is far more modest, and flexible dance wear is used.

The principal items that are worn are dresses, headwear and dance shoes, and each of these will be discussed in some detail in the next section, from the minimum requirements for a beginner up to a top championship dancer at a world championship. There are numerous suppliers available worldwide for the provision of dance wear. Lists of well-known suppliers or manufacturers of shoes, dresses and wigs are given in Appendix 1. Generally speaking, these can be purchased on line or at the suppliers' premises. In addition, the major suppliers attend the major feiseanna and competitions where they have stalls selling their merchandise.

Shoes

There are two types of shoe: soft shoes (also known as ghillies or pumps) and hard shoes. Hard shoes are similar to tap shoes, except that the tips and heels are made of fibreglass, instead of metal, and are significantly bulkier. The first hard shoes had wooden or leather taps with metal nails. Later the taps and heels were made of resin or fibreglass to reduce the weight and to make the sounds louder. The soft shoes are black lace-up shoes and are only worn by girls, while boys wear black leather shoes called 'reel shoes' with a hard heel. Boys' hard-shoe dancing features audible heel clicks. A new trend includes adding white laces to the soft shoes, and white tape to the straps of the hard shoes in order to give the illusion of elongating the legs. Photos of a range of soft and hard shoes are shown in the photographs.[14,15]

Weathered and worn – the steps along the road to success.

Costumes/Dresses

General

Irish dance schools generally have their own design of school dress worn by junior competitors, and for team competitions and in public performances. Each Irish dance school has its own distinctive full-skirted dress, often featuring lace or an embroidered pattern copied from medieval Irish patterns, especially on the collars and sleeves.

As dancers advance in competition or are given starring roles in public performances, they usually get a solo dress of their own design and colours or wear the team dress. In the 1970s and 1980s, ornately embroidered dresses became popular. Today even more ornamentation is used on girls'

Two choices of heavy shoe style.

Soft shoes.

Beginners' starter dresses.

A modern championship dress illustrating the move from Celtic motifs to the artistic use of diamantes in various shapes and colours.

A trendy gent's costume reflecting current fashions as worn by Josh Ruddock, Men's World Champion 2016.

dresses. Solo dress design is unique to each dancer.

Most men wear a shirt, vest and tie together with black trousers when competing. However, recent years have seen the introduction of jackets and tuxedos and waistcoats adorned with Celtic designs. Whilst black is still very popular, coloured ties and waistcoats are increasingly worn.

Costumes for Beginners, Classes and Rehearsals
Although ornate costumes are commonly worn at Irish dancing competitions, more modest and flexible costumes are used for classes and rehearsals, such as black tunics. It is likely that typical beginners and class dress will be as shown in the photos, with dancers in simple, plain dresses with straight hair, so that the footwork and movement of the dance is given complete focus.

More school dresses.

Dress for Solo Dancing Competition
As mentioned earlier, several generations ago the appropriate dress for a competition was simply 'Sunday best'. Since, then dress design has seen a major makeover. Dresses have become more and

Competition dresses: a view of the detail on the back of the dress.

more flexible and 'breathable' as compared to decades past, when tough material and elaborate decoration were usual. Competition dresses are designed to make the dancer look and feel their absolute best in the heat of the competition. At the top level, bespoke dresses are specifically tailored to the individual, with a personalized approach to the whole design process, measurements, manufacture and fitting. Dancers enjoy and benefit from this personal design consultation and private fittings. A professional makeover service is commonly offered at the final fitting, where dancers can also try out the latest Irish dance trends in make-up, wigs and unique hair accessories.[16]

Dress for Céilí Dancing

Dresses for céilí dancers are far more modest than for solo dancers and are usually based on the

Céilí World Champion Team 2009 – John Carey Academy.

school colours, style and emblems. A céilí team can consist of up to eight dancers, and whilst they are generally of a similar size and build, the dress selection needs to cater for a variety of dancer sizes.

Headwear

Headwear for Normal Classes

There are no specific rules for headwear at normal classes, although each school may have specific requirements – wigs and formal hairstyles are very rarely worn. Dancers simply wear what they are comfortable with, usually just their natural hairstyle or what the teacher requires.

Headwear for Competitions

Most dancers wear wigs for competitions. These are normally of two main types: bun wigs and full-length wigs. Bun wigs, not surprisingly, are bun shaped and typically sit on the back of the head over the dancer's normal hair or over a donut.

Full-length or short-style wigs usually come down to, but not below, the shoulder line and are available in varying lengths, depending on the height of the dancer. Younger dancers typically look better in medium-length full wigs. Both styles are worn by dancers of all ages, and the choice of which one to wear is a matter of personal preference. Céilí teams more often than not select the same type of wig, as this looks better on stage, providing an additional 'wow' and giving a more uniform appearance.

Hair donuts are made of lightweight sponge and are used by dancers who want additional height or volume in their wig. The dancer's natural hair is pulled into a small ponytail, and then threaded through the donut and pinned. This creates more bulk for the wig to sit on, so making the overall wig higher and fuller. Hair donuts are available in different sizes and in a number of different colours so dancers can match them to their normal hair colour, thus creating the effect they desire.

Different wigs have different styles of curl. The traditional Irish dance wigs have tighter ringlet curls, while other styles, such as the full-length wig or the bun wig, have a looser wave curl. Both styles are

A variety of wig colours and styles – up-style.

A variety of wig colours and styles – full one piece.

A variety of wig colours and styles – modern short style.

worn by dancers of all ages, so simply select the style you prefer. The photos illustrate examples of the traditional and the looser curl.

Other factors important in wig selection are wig colour and your own skin tone – a range of wig colours is available, and it is not essential that you match your own natural hair colour as you can spray-colour any exposed natural hair. The choice of colour also needs to complement your skin colour and the colour of your dress, both of which will matter on stage for a good overall effect; team dancers will also coordinate wig colours to look good on stage.[17]

Competition dancing is a very fast-moving activity so it is vital that the wig is kept securely in place. Wigs usually come with two combs, one at the front and one at the back to fix the wig through the dancer's natural hair. Some styles also come with elastic drawstrings for additional security. Bobby pins should be a key part of your feis bag: once the wig is fitted on the head use plenty of bobby pins to fix it securely in place – these come in different lengths, depending on what you need. Use U-shaped bobby pins if you need to fix through the wig; only use normal bobby pins on the side of the wig to clamp it on.

The whole process of fixing a wig can be stressful for new parents or dancers, but practice makes perfect; there are many videos on how to get a wig looking its best, and you can book a hair and make-up stylist at your feis.

Most dancers like to finish their headwear presentation with a tiara, headband or bow. This again is a personal choice. These can be obtained from a variety of vendors or from the vendor stalls at feiseanna.

Make-Up

The final part of the essential preparation for the female competition dancer is make-up. As detailed in most of the previous sections of this guide, it is advisable to seek professional help. As you progress through the competitive levels the stages change, the lights get brighter, the competition gets stronger, and as a consequence make-up requirements change. It is crucial to know how to make the most of your make-up for each individual stage and venue to ensure you look your best:[18] getting it wrong gets you noticed for the wrong reason.

Stage Make-Up

It is important that you wear the right type and amount of make-up. The object is to bring your face to life and to give you a happy look that will appeal to the judges. Understanding stage lighting is key.

One of the most important things about stage make-up is that its good effect lasts: you need to look attractive and great for the whole day, and you

A stunning example of a tiara used to crown a champion.

Make-up – the last touch-up.

need to be ready to go to your recall looking as fresh and dazzling as you did at 8:30 in the morning. When it comes to purchasing products, the key to its capacity to last all day is good quality. The purchase and use of good quality make-up, particularly for foundation and blush, is of paramount importance.

Bronzer is also important to counteract the washing-out effect of stage lights.

The following are some basic rules of stage make-up:

- Move away from colour matching your make-up, particularly bright eye shadow, to your dress – this practice is outdated now.
- The 'runway' look is in vogue – use more natural tones such as browns.
- Make your eyes appear very bright: avoid a lot of heavy mascara, eye shadow and eyeliner as this will distract from the natural colour and brightness of your eyes.
- Highlight the natural: when you do your make-up, smile so that you see the line of your cheek bones and can follow their natural line – this will lift your face. Don't paint on something that is not there naturally.

There are now a number of professional hair and make-up specialists who attend most major feiseanna and take bookings to give you that extra special look. A number currently practising commercially can be found on the internet.

THE RULES OF COMPETITIVE IRISH DANCING

As with most competitive dancing and sporting activities it is a fundamental requirement that every competition is governed by a set of rules. A summary of the major rules applicable to costumes, shoes and make-up for a CLRG registered competition is given below.[8] The other registered organizations use similar but not necessarily identical rules.

Costume Rules

Costumes or costuming is defined as any element of performance/presentation clothing worn by a dancer in the course of a competition, including, but not limited to, dress, waistcoat, trousers, shoes, headwear, capes, shawls, socks, underwear and make-up.

Costume Length

The length of costumes must adhere to the principles of modesty, and enable dancers to execute their movements and steps safely. Adjudicators who determine a costume to be too short or to lack modesty may ask a competitor to change into black tights in order for them to continue in the competition. When wearing body suits with skirts, black tights must be worn from the age of fourteen.

- Necklines must be at collarbone level or above. This does not preclude the use of alternative fabrics, for example lace, as an inset.
- Costumes must consist of full front, side and back sections, along with short/long sleeves. Cut-away styles, without a full skirt backing, are not acceptable.
- In order to protect dancers from hazardous objects on stage while competing, costumes may not be decorated with feathers.
- Dance drama costumes must be in keeping with the theme of the story portrayed.
- Competitors in all age groups, up to but excluding mean grad (Intermediate), may only wear traditional class costumes, or long-/short-sleeved blouses/polo tops and skirts/tunics that conform to the regular costume length rules as above. Low-cut tops and short, tight skirts are not permitted.
- Where chiffon or lace material is used as sleeves, the sleeves must start at the shoulder line and end at the cuff.
- Costumes for both boys and girls should not include representations such as globes, medals or any other item symbolic of an award having been achieved.
- Appropriate underwear, covering the midriff, must be worn. Where tights are worn, they must be of a denier of not less than 70.
- Body suits should be of premium fabric and should not show the body contour in detail. Recommended fabrics include velvet and lycra.
- Skirts worn over bodysuits should be the same length as full costumes and should sit at the dancer's mid-thigh at the back, with sufficient material to allow for movement when raising the leg. Tight sport skirts or gym skirts are not suitable. Wrap-around skirts should be secured with a pin.

- Costumes should have traditional themes; cartoon characters are not permitted.
- Female adult dancers participating in 'adult competitions' for both solos and teams are required to wear tights of a denier not less than 70.
- Boys'/men's costuming must adhere to principles of modesty, and should enable dancers to execute their movements and steps safely. Adjudicators who determine that a costume lacks modesty may use the 'Costume Infraction' programme in order to flag up the dancer and ensure the teacher is notified.

Make-Up

The following rules apply for the use of make-up.

- Make-up is not permitted for any dancer in the first two grades (Bungrád and Tusgrád or equivalent) up to and including the under-twelve age group worldwide.
- Make-up (including false eyelashes and tanner on the face) is not permitted for dancers, in either solo or team competitions, up to and including the under-ten age group.

Note: Both make-up rules refer to the age group of the competition, not the actual age of the dancer. For example, nine-year old dancers competing in a team that is entered in an 'Under 12' class may wear make-up, and at a feis where the youngest Open Championship age group is under eleven, then all dancers in that competition may wear make-up.

The Composition and Dimensions of Dancing Shoes

The following rules apply for the composition and construction of shoes:

- The heel and its 'top piece' must consist only of leather, leather composite, plastic or fibreglass, or a combination of these materials.
- The heel and its top piece must not contain any metal components or attachments other than

nails or screws to attach the heel to the shoe or the top piece to the heel.

- Where nails are used to attach the top piece to the heel they must not exceed 25 per cent of the total surface area of the top piece.
- The maximum permissible height of a heel from the surface of the top piece to the point where the heel joins the upper of the shoe is 1.5in (this height includes both heel and top piece and is measured to the back of the upper of the shoe).
- A certain amount of tapering from where the heel joins the upper of the shoe to where it joins the top piece is permissible (that is, the heel may be broader at the top than at the bottom) but such tapering must be at a constant angle – that is, the side of the heel must not be curved, and no protrusions from the side or back of the heel is allowed.
- It is possible, indeed probable, that in the future new construction techniques for shoes will evolve and/or new materials become available that will require a review of these directives. However, at no time in the future should new materials other than those listed above be used in shoes, nor any divergence from these directives introduced without prior authorization being sought from An Coimisiún.
- Any competitor found to be altering their shoes or wearing them on the wrong feet will be treated in the same manner as if using carriage aids, and will be subject to disqualification from that particular competition.

For heavy rounds in competitions, dancers may not wear soft shoes that have been altered with the addition of heels and tips in an attempt to turn them into hard shoes. Dancers found to be wearing such altered shoes for heavy rounds may be denied access to that round of the competition.

Mission accomplished!

CHAPTER 3

THE MUSIC OF THE DANCE

Music produces a kind of pleasure which human nature cannot do without.

Confucius

Irish music has grown hand in hand with Irish dancing throughout the centuries, and it is difficult to know which actually came first! Its roots would lie with the Druids in pre-Christian times, but much of what we know as 'trad' music would have originated in the eighteenth century. It was very popular at weddings and other social events, and up to the beginning of the early twentieth century it was common practice for dance masters to travel the country with a fiddle player or piper in tow. Even as recently as 1950, dancing at the crossroads was a favourite pastime in rural Ireland.

IRISH DANCE MUSICIANS AND BANDS

In more recent times Irish dance music is often heard in a concert environment, to be listened to rather than danced to, and this can affect the speed at which dances are played, rather than the stricter speeds set at competition – for example a hornpipe will not necessarily be played at dance speed – and today's musicians like to play at fast speeds to excite their audiences.

Céilí bands started quite recently in the early part of the twentieth century, usually with a fiddle, accordion and snare drum. The first céilí was organized in London in 1897 by the Gaelic League, but band size gradually increased up to ten musicians, and instruments included the flute, banjo, uilleann pipes and piano. As the popularity of these increased throughout Ireland, England and America, more players would be added so the music could be heard by everyone over the noise of many dancers in a large hall – even saxophone players were employed for big occasions.

Dances for these céilíthe would include jigs, quadrille sets, waltzes and hornpipes, among others. Their popularity soon came to the notice of the government, and in 1937 the Dance Halls Act was passed: this outlawed dancing outside, and a licence had to be obtained and the céilí had to take place in a parish hall. Public demand for the music meant that radio stations regularly played it in the 1930s and 1940s, and this was maintained by the Fleadh Cheoil in the 1950s.

One of the first céilí bands to gain international success was the Ballinakill Céilí Band, which was formed in 1927 under their parish priest Fr Larkin. They recorded for Radio Eireann in 1929, and the following year went to London to record four tunes. This recording became an unexpected hit, and they went on to record six double-sided records by 1931, with sales in the tens of thousands. They achieved international fame, and went on to influence many other bands right up to the 1960s.

Another very popular band is the Kilfenora Céilí Band, formed in County Clare in 1910 and still going strong today. They won the All-Ireland Fleadh Cheoil three years in a row in the mid-1950s, and tickets were sold out in large venues all over the UK. They even have a museum dedicated to them in the Burren Centre, Kilfenora – in fact this is the only

OPPOSITE: **Lord of the Dance fiddlers in action.**

museum in the world designed for living artists. As recently as 2015 they recorded their highly successful album 'Now is the Hour' – proof that céilí music is alive and well.

INSTRUMENTS

The main instruments used to play Irish music are the accordion, fiddle, the uilleann pipes, the flute, tin whistle, bodhran and harp. Others can include the banjo, the low whistle, the concertina, bouzouki, piano and guitar, the last two used for providing rhythmical accompaniment. From the tenth to the seventeenth century the harp was the most dominant of these, as harpists were employed by the ruling princes of Ireland to create and play music for them. The most famous of these early harpists was the blind O'Carolyn, whose pieces are still played today. This system changed in 1607 when the Irish princes were forced to flee; this hugely affected

A typical traditional fiddle as used for Irish dance music.

the harpists' tradition, and they became 'travelling' players.[5]

The fiddle: Perhaps the most famous instrument associated with Irish music is the fiddle. This actually had its origins in Italy in the seventeenth century before its use spread all over Europe. In Ireland each county would have had its own particular style, with some of the greatest exponents of the 1920s including James Morrison, Paddy Killoran and Michael Coleman, all of whom came from County Sligo; in the 1950s and 1960s there was the great Sean Maguire from Belfast, and Larry Mathews from County Kerry.

The tin whistle: Of the wind instruments, the tin whistle – or penny whistle, as it was commonly known, because it was used by the beggars in Dublin – is the highest pitched. Its cousin the low whistle is just a larger version but is lower pitched and has a mellower sound. The wooden flute is

An early model of the Irish harp.

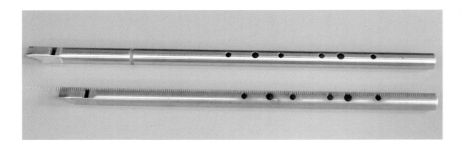

Simple whistles.

An early button accordion.

The accordion: This instrument arrived in Ireland in the latter half of the nineteenth century, and both the piano-keyed and button-keyed models remain very popular in both céilí and competition dancing. There are various tunings for the button key – B/C and C#/D – and this can influence the style of music played. In the 1940s and 1950s Joe Burke, Sonny Brogan and Paddy O'Brien were all noted players, and more recently Sharon Shannon, Charlie Piggot and Johnny O'Leary, amongst others.

The bodhran: This is an old drum but a relatively young musical instrument, and although it has existed in Ireland for centuries it really only became part of traditional music in the 1960s and 1970s. It is made of animal skin stretched over a circular wooden frame and played with a wooden beater. It provides a great rhythmical accompaniment to the main instrument, although in céilí it is usually replaced by a snare drum and in competition dancing by a piano to provide 'vamping' accompaniment to whichever tune is being played.

A piano accordion.

An example of a bodhran drum.

quite unique to Ireland and has a velvety sound – Matt Molloy of the Chieftains is one of its greatest exponents.

One of the hardest instruments to play – the uilleann pipes.

The uilleann pipes: One of the hardest instruments to learn and play is the uilleann pipes. There have been pipes used in Irish music for many centuries, but it was by the middle of the nineteenth century that modern-day pipes took shape as we hear them today. Some of the great players have been Seamus Ennis, Paddy Maloney, Liam O'Flynn and more recently Davy Spillane.[5]

COMPOSITION

Irish dance music is usually composed in patterns of bar-long melodic phrases similar to call and response. A common pattern would consist of A and B parts played twice each time with four- to eight-bar phrases, and the entire tune played three times – for example AABB AABB AABB, with embellishments or ornamentation usually on the last section including slides, rolls, cuts and trills. Up until 1792, when Edward Bunting made the first attempt to write down these tunes for posterity, they would have been passed down aurally from generation to generation, and it would have required an excellent memory to recall several hundred tunes on request. They were later published in 1840 as *The Ancient Music of Ireland*.

The majority of Irish jigs are native in origin and were composed by pipers and fiddlers such as Seamus Ennis, Micho Russell and Leo Rowsome. However, some were adapted from English and Scottish tunes. The Fairy Reel was composed in Scotland in 1802 but became popular in Ireland a century later. Most composers would look around them for inspiration – for example The Garden of Daisies, Harvest Home and Stack of Barley. Some were inspired by political events: for example Bonaparte's Retreat, which was written in about 1798 when a French invasion was expected to help overthrow English rule.

In recent times, the internet and the worldwide success of Riverdance and Lord of the Dance has prompted more interest in new compositions; this has also been motivated commercially by an increase in publishing royalties. As a result of this and digital recording services, which enable the speed and manner of transmission, these newly composed tunes are spreading across the world at a faster rate than ever before.

Another factor was the rapid economic growth in Ireland in the early 1990s known as the Celtic Tiger. This phenomenon gave the country a more visible cultural presence on the world stage. A country situated on the periphery of Europe now experienced an influx and outflux of musical influence, thus leading to a non-Irish slant on new composition. This also applied to America with Cape Breton fiddle and Appalachian music. Accordionist John Kimmel, son of German immigrants living in New York, was highly respected and influential among Irish musicians and his style would translate to new tunes and the way they were played. These new compositions may enter into common practice through modern-day media quite quickly, but it will take many years to show they have stood the test of time to attain the reverence of the older tunes.

RHYTHM AND MUSICAL STRUCTURE

For solo competition dances there are eight dance styles musically speaking: the reel, the slip jig, the light jig and the 'single jig' (also referred to as a hop jig) danced in soft shoe, while heavy jig, hornpipe, traditional set and open set are danced in heavy shoe.

Reels have a 4/4 time signature and a speed of 113 beats per minute for open dancers, or 122–124 for beginners.

Slip jigs are in 9/8 time with a speed similar to the reel, depending on whether they are open or beginner.

Light and single jigs are in 6/8 time, with a different emphasis within the measure distinguishing the music at speeds of 116 and 120.

Hard shoe dances include the hornpipe in syncopated 4/4 time, the treble jig (also called the 'heavy jig' or 'double jig') in a slow 6/8 time, the treble reel (hard shoe dance done to reel music) and 'traditional sets', which are a group of dances with set music and steps. Many traditional sets have irregular musical phrasing. There are also more advanced 'non-traditional sets' performed by advanced dancers. These have set music, but not steps. There are multiple traditional sets, including St Patrick's Day, Blackbird, Job of Journeywork, Three Sea Captains, Garden of Daisies, King of the Fairies and Jockey to the Fair.

Competitive dancers generally dance two or three steps at a time, depending on their dancing level. Each step lasts for sixteen bars of music, eight bars per step. They are each danced starting with the right foot for eight bars, then repeated with the left foot for the last eight bars, doing the same movements with the opposite feet. Set dances, however, have a different format. The dancer usually dances one step, which is a set number of bars (which can vary), and is then repeated, resembling the steps of other dances. Then the dancer usually dances a 'set', which is not repeated. It is a highly sought after and competitive feat to dance this 'third round' – at regional, national and world competitions only a small percentage (typically the top half of dancers graded after the first two rounds) of dancers are invited back to perform. Popular set dances are Planxty Davis, Kilkenny Races,

Drunken Gauger and more recently The Vanishing Lake.

The céilí dances used in competitions are more precise versions of those danced in less formal settings. There is a list of thirty céilí dances that have been standardized and published in *An Coimisiún's Ár Rincí Céilí* (*see* Chapter 5 for more detail) as examples of typical Irish folk dances; these include Trip to the Cottage, High Caul Cap, Cross Reel, Eight-Hand Jig, Eight-Hand Reel and St Patrick's Day. Most Irish dancing competitions only ask for a short piece of any given dance, in the interests of time.

It is one thing to be able to perform these dances technically correctly and in time, and both these are essential to achieve the best marks in competition; however, another factor is the natural musicality that some dancers have. To some it seems as natural as breathing, while to others it can remain a mystery. Everybody can hear the same music differently, and each dancer can interpret that music in their own way, and that reflects in the way they dance. This is something that can't really be taught, but is more of a 'feel' thing. As the great dancer Colin Dunne has said: 'Sometimes it's not just all about how fast I can click or how high I can kick, but finding another connection to the movement and the rhythm of the dance.'

Raising the roof – a quartet of fiddlers blowing up a storm in Celtic Tiger.

CHAPTER 4

SOLO DANCING

Every dance you make belongs to you. It is part of your collection. When you think of it like that, you'll want to make your next routine the best you've ever made.

Torron-Lee Dewar

The first three chapters have discussed the history of Irish dance and music, and also its meteoric rise and some of the more recent developments and innovations. The key actions on the path to becoming an Irish dancer have been explored: selecting a school, acquiring an instruction manual, and buying new dance shoes and class gear. So now to the really exciting part: learning the Irish dance steps and routines. The next two chapters will concentrate on dancing itself, starting with solo dancing.

Solo dancing is an extremely complex and vast topic, and to help clarify its detail and complexities this chapter will be split into two parts: Part One describes the basic and traditional steps used in Irish dancing, and shows how these steps and core movements are used to choreograph dance routines. It will also demonstrate how to dance the following dances: the reel, the light jig, the single jig, slip jig, heavy jig, treble jig and the hornpipe.

Once these have been mastered, Part Two will study some of the more progressive steps and traditional set dances. In addition we will look at choreographing a non-traditional set dance, and will explore the musical and dance development of two recently approved new set dances: the Vanishing Lake and the Charlady.

PART ONE: THE FUNDAMENTALS AND BASIC STEPS IN SOLO DANCING

OVERVIEW

The full dance teaching programme that is required in order to become a championship-level Irish dancer is both complex and takes many years to complete. Therefore before detailing the steps of the individual dances, the overall teaching programme that is typically followed from beginner to champion needs to be explained.

Dance Structure

Teachers and dancers may count bars of music and dance steps slightly differently to musicians. For example:

- In reel time an ordinary one, two, three or a skip two, three equals one bar of music.
- In 6/8 time (jig time) the 'rising step' in any of its forms equals one bar.
- In heavy shoe treble jig, treble, treble, hop back two, three, four equals one bar.
- In hornpipe 4/4 time, tip and tip and treble hop back equals one bar.

This will be explained in more detail in the individual sections for each dance. Most dances consist of four main basic movements:

- A lead around: a total of eight bars in basic dance, usually sixteen in advanced dances.
- The sidestep (sevens): a total of eight bars in basic dance, omitted in advanced dances.
- First step right and left: total sixteen bars.
- Second step right and left: total sixteen bars.

These feature in various forms in the reel, light jig, single jig, slip jig and heavy jig, especially in beginners' grades. The hornpipe is slightly different in that it starts with a lead up, rather than a lead around, followed by the first step, performed on the right foot and then the left, then the second step, which is usually only danced on the right foot. This gives a total of forty bars for the hornpipe. These movements are taught sequentially, in the following sections, at increasingly difficult levels.

Performance Levels

Initially dances are taught at beginner level, then as the dancer becomes more competent the dances become progressively more difficult as additional features are added. A typical range for, say, a reel would be:

1. Basic.
2. Primary.
3. Preliminary.
4. Open Advanced.
5. Championship.

Competitions are held at these levels at feisianna and international events, as will be explained in Chapter 6.

The Teaching Process

As has been said, most Irish dances are choreographed from a number of different step sequences that we can call the core and/or basic movements. These are used in the various dance routines, depending on the performance level. The core movements that need to be learnt are commonly known as:

- The basic threes, the sevens, then progressing on to:

- Rocks.
- Boxes.
- Cross keys.
- Clicks – as difficulty increases, they become doubles and triples.
- Up and overs.
- The Bird – a more recent movement.
- The Butterfly – a more recent movement.

These are of increasing complexity. Beginners are initially taught the threes and sevens that are required for the simpler dances. As dancers become more proficient, they progress through the levels to the more complex elements and dances that will follow. However, before tackling the first steps we will look at the fundamentals of body deportment – a crucial first step in an Irish dancing career.

DEPORTMENT, POSTURE AND STARTING POSITION

Before starting on teaching the basic steps and movements, it is important to describe and highlight the nature and importance of deportment/posture, and the starting position. It is recommended that the student dancer returns to this section as a reminder before the commencement of each new dance, especially for those learning the basic beginner dances.

Posture

Irish dancing is unique as compared to any other dance genre because in competitive and traditional solo dancing it is performed with the arms held down in a straight line by the body sides, not stiffly but in a relaxed manner, with no bend in the arm. This is the traditional manner for solo dancing, and to this day it is still performed competitively this way. This will be discussed more fully later in the chapter. However, in the sections on show dancing in chapters 1, 7 and 8, it can be seen how changes came about, especially by Michael Flatley in Riverdance and Lord of the Dance. This is the biggest difference in Irish dance format in the last twenty-five

Arm position viewed from the front.

Arm position viewed from the side.

Full body line from head to toe.

Starting position for competitive solo dancing for all levels. Note the stretch and pull on both legs.

Feet position: with the heels together showing the ankles and feet turned out.

Feet position: turned out from front and back.

Now check the full line from head to feet.

years. It is frequently asked 'How do you keep your balance with your arms down by your side?' It is a skill in itself that comes with constant practice!

Body Line and Feet Position

Regarding the line of the body and the feet positions, the photos show the line of the body from head to toe, and in particular the position of the head, shoulders, hips and knees and the position of the feet. The head is in line with the shoulders and the rest of the body, not jutting out or tilted up. The shoulders are in a straight line across with a slight pull at the back, drawing the bones at the back towards each other, while the hips are also in a straight line across, neither one turned slightly out, forwards or back.

Now to the knees: the right leg is in front of the left, with no open space between them, slightly pulled (in a locked position) facing to the front. In many other dance genres the knees are turned out more. It is important to keep that pull and stretch on the knee, keeping the knees closed and stretched whilst dancing.

The photos show the position of the feet, with the right foot in front; this position/angle remains the same whichever foot is in front. Remember this is for basic steps – sometimes there are slight variations in very advanced competitive and show style dancing, which will be covered in later chapters. The feet must be turned out at all times, both the *front and back foot.* The ankles should be seen from the front at all times: the front foot should have the heel lined up in front, slightly covering the back foot *with toes turned out* and the foot at an angle of approximately 45 degrees. Check in a mirror that the front ankle and back ankle can be seen from the front. Now check from the top down: the top line head, shoulders, hips, lower line knees (no space) and the line of the feet front and back.

The Starting Position

The starting position is that taken at the commencement of every dance, especially in solo competitions. At the start of each dance refer to the starting position above for guidance. In show dancing this varies according to the dance and the choreography.

The following are basic exercises to help build turnout and placement into training routines.

Exercise One

Stand with the feet side by side, put the heels together, balancing on both feet in front of a full-length mirror. From this position put down the right leg/foot in front of the left foot, and balance on both feet again: this is count one: check in the mirror that the feet are in the correct position – the right heel in front of the left toe at 45 degrees.

Now lift the right foot again, balance on the left foot, take the right foot to a standing position; put your weight again on both feet, and both heels together in line with the ankles facing front: this is count two.

Still working the right foot, bring it behind the left foot, transfer your weight to the left foot again, putting the toe of the right foot behind the heel of the left foot, with both feet still turned out; check in the mirror that both ankles can be seen. The weight is now on both feet again: this is count three.

For the last count bring the right foot back again to heels together and in line, with both feet weight bearing: this is count four.

Remember, as you move the leg/foot, the rest of the body (top part) is *not to turn or move with you*: the shoulders or hips must remain facing the front without turning.

Each count is done to one bar of reel music, 4/4 time signature: the first four counts using the right foot will take four bars of music. Then exactly the same movement is started using the left leg/foot in a mirror image, following the same rules.

Now try it with the music counting, standing with the heels together and the weight on both feet:

1. Right foot in front for one.
2. Together for two.
3. Right behind for three.
4. Together for four.
5. Left foot in front for five.
6. Together for six.
7. Behind for seven.
8. Together for eight.

Exercise 1: Starting position with the heels together.

1. **Right foot** in front for **one**.

2. Feet together for **two**.

3. Right foot behind for **three**.

4. Feet together for **four**.

5. Left foot in front for **five**.

6. Feet together for **six**.

7. Left foot behind for **seven**.

8. Feet together for **eight**.

Exercise Two

This exercise should help with line and balance. Count each lift and point to one bar of reel music. The standing position is the same as in the first exercise. Facing the mirror, check out the line from head to toe. To count one, lift the right foot to the level of the back knee, check that the toe is pointed and the foot turned out, and squeeze the toes; the balance is on the left foot: count up for one, now lower it to the floor and point it on the floor. Count point for two, up for three, point for four: continue up to and include eight. Your balance remains on your left foot for the eight bars, lifting, pointing and squeezing the toes.

Now switch and practise this balance drill using your left foot to lift and point and balancing on your right foot, for eight bars of music, squeezing the toes of the working leg.

These two exercises should be done after each warm-up, before starting to dance. Repeat them for approximately ten minutes. They are very good for posture, placement and balance.

Posture and Balance

Posture and balance are essential necessities in Irish dancing: it is impossible to perform correctly without them. The straight line of the body with the arms down by the body side is unique to Irish solo dancing.

Each step or movement is meant to be performed without it affecting the carriage/posture. For example, when performing a jump, leap or click, or any elevated movement, the top part of the body should not move out of alignment, either by leaning forwards or backwards or jerking, and the arms should remain straight down by the side, neither lifting, bending nor moving out. No sign of stress, strain or effort should be evident in any of the steps or movements.

When dancing it is important to maintain balance – many other dancing genres find it difficult to maintain balance dancing with the arms down by the side. Having good balance gives you control of yourself to transfer weight from one foot to the other and to execute the step or dance correctly. Another

Exercise 2: 1. Point for **one.**

2. Up to the knee for **two.**

Bad posture: leaning forwards.

Bad posture: leaning back.

important skill in dance is to dance in time with the music, and good balance is a great help with this.

DANCE TERMS

Similar to other dancing genres, hobbies and sports, Irish dancing has unique words that are used to describe various aspects of the dance and movements employed in the execution and instruction of the dancing steps and movements. The table on p. 60 lists a number of terms, frequently used throughout the guide, that the beginner may not be familiar with, together with a brief explanation of their meaning.

BASIC AND TRADITIONAL STEPS FOR BEGINNERS

The Basic Threes and Sevens – The Easy Reel

Beginners are initially taught the threes and sevens that are required for the simpler dances. These two very basic steps are usually taught as an introduction to Irish dancing and are commonly known as 'the threes' and 'the sevens' (or sidestep). These are the foundation of all Irish dances, whether for a light shoe or heavy shoe, solo dancing, ceílí dancing or figure choreography.

GLOSSARY OF SOLO IRISH DANCING TERMS

Word	Explanation
Reel	A dance with the most common tune type in 4/4 time. Usually performed in a soft shoe.
Jig	One of the oldest dances in a number of different types such as light jig, double jig, slip jig – written in 6/8, 12/8 and 9/8 time. Can be danced in either a soft or heavy shoe.
Hornpipe	A dance in heavy shoe in 4/4 or 2/4 time.
Lead around	The first eight or sixteen bars in a solo step dance. The dancer usually moves in a circle in a clockwise or anticlockwise direction.
Sidestep	A single move horizontally to the right and then to the left between the lead around and the first step.
First step	Usually danced eight bars on the right foot then eight bars on left, mirroring the same movements/steps.
Second step	As for the first step.
Bar	A unit into which a piece of music can be divided.
Count	Each step or part of a step is broken down into specific counts.
Point	Squeezing the toes of the working foot – making an arch, with the heel raised off the floor.
Time signature	Tells you how the music is to be counted. It is written at the beginning of the staff after the clef and key signature. It consists of two numbers written like a fraction (for example 4/4). The top number defines how many beats there are, and the lower number what kind of beats they are: in 4/4 the top (first) number indicates that there are four beats in each measure, and the bottom (second) number indicates that there are four crotchets in each measure.
Drill	A drill breaks down a step or dance into small sections so it can be practised over and over again until it is perfect.
Rock	A traditional movement in Irish solo dancing.
Cross keys	A traditional movement in Irish solo dancing.
Box	A traditional movement in Irish solo dancing.
Click	An elevated solo movement when the dancer is suspended in mid-air and one leg passes the other with the heels meeting and clicking while in suspension.
Solo set dance	A dance that is danced in a heavy shoe. It consists of two parts: part A is referred to as the 'lead up' and is performed on the right and left foot. The bars for this can vary and are usually shorter than those in the second part, part B, which is called 'the set' and is danced on the right foot only. (Set dances and social set dancing will be explained later in this chapter.)
Beat	A beat or count of music.

The Threes

When a beginner, regardless of age, commences lessons they are usually taught the 'one-two-threes' first. It is the beginning of the first dance, known as 'the easy reel' or (basic reel), which is danced to 4/4 time signature, four crotchets to a bar, and they are danced to eight bars of music (8×3s). The first movement is usually called 'the lead around', when eight threes are danced in a circle in a clockwise or anticlockwise direction, moving comfortably in all directions. There are two versions of the threes: the first is referred to as 'the ordinary threes' (jump threes) and the second is called 'the skip threes'. In this guide we will work with the ordinary or jump threes.

The One-Two-Threes in Slow Motion (Ordinary Threes)

This is the step-forward version of the jump threes. Stand with the right foot in front, and the right heel in front and covering the back foot at 45 degrees – it should also be possible to draw a line from the little toe of the right foot straight back to the left heel.

Stand tall, elongating the body and stretching all the way up, then lift the right foot keeping the weight and balance on the back left foot, pulling up on the toes of the back foot, and squeezing and pointing the right foot. Take a step forwards with the right foot, now put it down on the floor in front of you, transferring your weight on to it (count one beat).

Now the left foot is lifted up: bring it forwards in front of the right foot (the same motion as if you were walking) and put it down in front of the right foot, transferring the weight on to it. Lift up the right foot, which is now at the back (count second beat): now put the right foot down at the back (behind), transferring the weight on to it (count third beat).

That is the one-two-three step and count, which equals one bar of music. The left foot is now in front, and you are bearing your weight on your right foot.

Now start the one-two-three process again from here, leading with the left foot. Continue until eight have been completed. An easy way to say it, especially for younger people, is walk, walk, up at the back (and then put it down at the back), continue with the next foot, completing each three until you have completed eight. Remember to be on your toes or the ball of both feet throughout (with the heels raised up off the floor).

One-two-threes: **1. Step forwards with the right foot.**

2. Raise the left foot up at the back.

3. Step forwards with the left foot.

4. Put the left foot down in front, raising the right foot up at the back.

Initially it is done in a slow walking mode, but as you gain confidence and competence in the movement you can add a little bounce and jump as you transfer weight on to each foot. The more you practise with the music, counting each three to a bar of music, the more your timing and rhythm will improve.

As mentioned above there are two formats of 'the threes' – the above is the 'ordinary threes', while below is the second format, referred to as 'skip threes'. Both are accepted in basic solo dances and in céilí dances in competition, where it enables a team to move and travel forwards in a smoother manner. The second format 'skip threes' is mainly favoured.

Skip Threes
Take up the starting position as before. With the right foot in front and the weight on the back foot, lightly raise the right foot and hop, keeping it raised, and extending it out in front for one count, keeping

the toe pointed. On the count of one put it down in front of you and transfer your weight on to it, lifting the back foot up behind (the left foot). The right foot will remain in front for the next two counts. Now put the left foot down again behind you for a count of two, transferring the weight on to it; then raise the right foot in front. For the count of three put the right foot down again in front, transferring the weight on to it while lifting the left foot up behind you.

That completes the first 'skip three' (one bar of music); continue alternating the feet until eight have been completed – that accounts for eight bars of music, be it reel or jig time. The main difference between the two is that in ordinary threes you first step down in front with the right foot, putting weight on it, while in skip threes the first move is with the weight on the back foot (the left foot), then hop and skip forwards with the right foot before placing it down in front putting weight on it. As in the ordinary threes, practise the skip threes in a similar manner in

Skip threes: 1. Raise the right foot in front, hopping with the left foot.

2. Put the right foot down in front, raising the left foot at the back.

3. Place the left foot down at the back, raising the right foot in front.

4. Put the right foot down in front, raising the left foot at the back.

all directions, until it can be performed smoothly and easily to music, keeping the heels raised off the floor.

The Sevens

The next step is called 'the sevens' or 'sidestep', and is performed to the next eight bars of music, first to the right for seven counts, then two threes are danced. The seven steps and two threes take four bars of music, then return by taking seven steps to the left followed by 'two threes', which is another four bars – making eight bars in total for the side-step. Sometimes the sidestep is performed going to the left first, and then returning (eight bars).

In the easy reel (basic reel) there is usually another step added after this, and it is performed on the right foot for eight bars and then replicated on the left foot for eight bars. Each school has its own variations for this, consisting of different combinations of threes, sevens and heel.

As dancers learn to move freely using these different variations, they become more proficient at changing feet, moving in different directions, counting with the music and learning to keep their balance.

The Sevens in Slow Motion

The sevens is also the foundation of most solo and ceílí dances. It is also known as 'the sidestep', which the official handbook of *An Coimisiún le Rincí Gaelacha* describes thus: 'The sidestep is the basis of all Irish dances and must be mastered before the dances can be executed with any degree of grace.'[19]

The sidestep is still in reel time, and is usually performed after the eight threes are performed in the basic solo reel and throughout ceílí dances in reel time. Standing upright and elongating the body, place the right foot in front of the left, with the ankles turned out and the heel in front of the left toe, and raise the right foot to knee height; then balancing on the left foot and keeping the right foot raised, hop for one count. Now put the right foot on the ground taking a little step to the right, and transfer the weight on to the right foot keeping it in front, for the count of two. The left foot is raised up behind, but now put the left foot down behind for count three.

With the weight now on it, again keeping the right foot in front and taking a small step to the right, put it down for the count of four; continue in this manner up to the count of seven. Remember to keep the right foot in front all the way up to and including the count of seven, transferring your weight each time with each count.

You have now taken seven steps to the right, and your weight is now on your left foot, which is at the back. That has taken two bars of music. For the next two bars of music dance the first basic step twice from above – the basic one-two-three step, which is called 'two threes'; now refer to the instructions earlier on 'ordinary threes' and perform them here.

Having just performed two one-two-threes of the first basic step, which took another two bars of music, your right foot is in front, and your weight is on your left foot behind you. Now return to the starting place to your left, bring your right foot to the back and place it down behind you, and put your weight on it for the count of one. Keep your left foot in front for the count of seven, alternating your weight from front to back with each count till you reach seven. To complete, dance as before two threes, then starting with the left foot in front, step two threes, then the right foot, then step two threes. This completes the sevens/the sidestep in reel time.

- Seven to the right takes two bars of music.
- Two one-two-threes (two jump two threes) takes two bars of music.
- Seven returning to the left takes two bars of music.
- Two one-two-threes (two jump two threes) takes two bars of music, which takes eight bars of music.

You now have the lead around for eight bars, the sevens/sidestep for eight bars, which is usually followed by another step with combinations of the above: threes, sevens, and heels danced on the right foot for eight bars, then mirrored on the left foot for eight bars.

The Light Jig

Now that you have learnt the first basic solo beginner reel we will move on to the next basic dance,

Sevens/sidestep: 1. Raise the right foot above the back knee and hop with the left foot for **one**.

2. Put the right foot down in front, lifting the left foot up at the back for **two**.

3. Put the left foot down at the back, raising the right foot in front for **three**.

4. Put the right foot down in front, lifting the left foot at the back for **four**.

5. Put the left foot down at the back, raising the right foot in front for **five**.

6. Put the right foot down in front, lifting the left foot at the back for **six**.

which is called the 'light jig' or 'light double jig'. This is danced in jig time, which is 6/8 time and is also danced in light shoes. It comprises a lead around, eight bars repeated, performed moving in an anti-clockwise direction, eight bars taking you to the halfway point, which is usually front of stage, then continue in the same direction to complete the circle and return to the starting place for the second eight bars. (You may perform it in a clockwise direction if you are more comfortable with that: the same principle is applied.) One of the more popular steps used for the lead around is described below.

In class this dance is usually taught as the second basic dance. It takes the dancer from basic reel rhythm to jig rhythm, in 6/8 time.

The Starting Position

Start by taking up the starting position as explained at the beginning of the chapter. From here on this will be referred to as the 'starting position' when introducing each solo dance. It is the starting position for all solo dances, from beginners to advanced

7. Put the left foot down at the back, raising the right foot in front for **seven**.

levels and especially in competitive solo dancing, be it light or heavy shoe. This is the traditional position; in show dancing it is more variable.

The Lead Around

A common variation of a lead around in a light jig is danced as follows. In the first bar of music, hop with the left foot three times before putting the right foot down on the floor; this means your weight and balance is on the left foot throughout, as outlined below:

- First hop: bend the right knee and raise the right foot in front to the height of the back knee with the toe pointed.
- Second hop: hop with the left foot, keeping the right foot raised: bring it to the inside of the left knee, and continue bringing it back, tucking it up to your bottom.
- Third hop: hop again with the left foot, with the right foot still raised, then bring it to the front as in the first hop. Now stretch it out in front and put it down in front for the count of one, lifting the left foot up at the back. Place the left foot down at the back for the count of two, raising the right foot, which is still in front. Put the right foot down again in front for the count of three.

The count from the start goes like this:

- Hop, hop, hop, one two three: this takes two bars – the left foot is now up behind you and your weight is on the right foot.
- Repeat the same movement commencing with the left foot: this takes two bars.
- Now repeat the same movement again with the right foot: this takes two bars. The total equals six bars.
- For the last two bars dance the rising step, as explained in Chapter 5 (*see* instructions for the rising step in céilí section).

This completes eight bars. Now repeat the eight bars starting on the left foot and continuing to the original position. This is the sixteen-bar lead around.

Lead around in light jig: 1. Raise the right leg above the back knee, hopping with the left foot – first hop.

2. Hop again with the left foot, bringing the right leg behind and up – second hop.

3. Hop again with the left foot, bringing the right foot to the front – third hop.

The Second Step (Sidestep) in the Light Double Jig
Starting Position
Raise the right foot, toe pointed, with the weight on the left foot, then hop with the left foot. Now moving slightly to the right, place the right foot down in front on the ball of the foot, for one count: your weight is now on the right foot and the left foot is raised behind.

Hop and bring the left foot to kick the right foot with the toe of the left foot, and keeping the left foot raised, hop back, and place the left foot down behind, transferring your weight.

The right foot is now raised: hop with the left foot, bringing the right foot back on the hop – place it down behind counting one, two, three, four, transferring the weight with each count (in a rocking manner). The right foot has remained at the back for those counts.

You can say the above piece matching the words and the feet together like this:

Hop down, kick, hop back, hop back two, three, four: this takes two bars. Repeat this twice more, making six bars.

For the last two bars the famous 'rising step' is danced: this will often occur in ceílí dances in 6/8 time (*see* Chapter 5: the instructions for this are in the notes under the definition of rising step). For the last two bars of the sidestep in the light double jig, dance the rising step on the right foot. This completes the eight bars. The step is then danced starting with the left foot, mirroring each piece of the right foot's eight bars (making a total of sixteen bars).

Sometimes another sixteen bars are performed, eight bars with the right foot and repeated on the left foot for eight bars: this is a combination of the first two steps and variations of the rising step (refer to the ceílí section).

The Single Jig

The next recommended solo dance to learn is the single jig, as it is also danced in 6/8 time signature. A very popular tune – especially for children to remember and perform to – is Pop Goes the Weasel, or 'hump-ty dump-ty'. In the single jig the predominant rhythm is a crotchet followed by a quaver.

The single jig 6/8 time signature is two sets of dotted quarter notes plus eight notes, such as 'hump-ty dump-ty'. Crotchets are interspersed with quavers.

The double jig 6/8 time signature is two sets of three eight notes, such as 'hip-pet-y hop-pet-y', where every quaver is sounded.

A Simple Lead Around for the Basic Single Jig
The starting position is as explained for the basic or easy reel. Point the toe and take a step with the right foot: transfer your weight to it and hop, raising the left foot and counting step and hop (now your weight is on the right foot with the left foot raised). Repeat the same step with the left foot and raise the right foot: transfer the weight as before, and hop.

Continue repeating and alternating the feet until you have done it six times and you have the right foot raised with the weight on the left foot at the back. Make a little jump to switch feet and weight: now the left foot is in front, and keep it in front for the last two bars, counting switch two, three, in front of the right foot. It is now slightly out to your left for a count of two beats – four, five – then the last two counts six, seven, are in front of the right foot. Remember to transfer the weight with each count and beat. Each odd beat – three, five, seven – is done with the back foot, the count being switch two, three, four, five, six, seven. That completes eight bars. Now continue your circle to the starting place for eight bars.

The direction of the circle is usually clockwise, but it can be performed anticlockwise if preferred.

Sidestep for a Single Jig

The sidestep takes eight bars on the right foot, then repeat on the left foot. Raise the right foot toes down and pointed, take a step to your right for one, then follow with your left foot behind for two. Bend and raise your right knee to the level of the back knee and hop with your left foot twice. The count for this is step and step and hop and hop: repeat three times in all, finishing with the same ending step as in the lead around above (switching feet two, three, four, five, six, seven). The left foot is now in front, and you repeat the same eight bars mirrored on the left foot.

The challenge is now to choreograph another eight bars and repeat on the left foot, incorporating the steps from your lead around and sidestep above, not forgetting the ending piece, which is quite typical to the single jig and emphasizes the beat and rhythm.

The Slip Jig Danced in 9/8 Signature Time

Overview

The slip jig is performed in all grades including championships and major events. It is danced in a unique time signature of 9/8 and is very popular in Irish dancing. It is mainly performed by females, although if you are in a class you will see boys learning it too. This is mainly to learn the musical interpretation and steps. They do not usually perform it on stage, after the basic form, which is performed in the beginner grades at competitions. They must also learn it for their grade examinations in both the basic and advanced form and if they are taking their TCRG examination. Although it is mainly a soft shoe dance, it can also be used for hard shoe, as in the set dance 'Is the Big Man Within?', which is 9/8 and 6/8 time signatures.

The slip jig is a very beautiful, graceful dance and my favourite soft shoe dance. I was inspired at a very young age by a Northern Irish dance teacher and choreographer, Patricia Mulholland, who taught and choreographed in the organization called The Festivals. I first saw a choreographed slip-jig group of hers on Telefís Eireann (Irish national television) in the 1960s. Her choreography has inspired me to this day, both in competitions and in show performances.

In a slip jig you should glide and flow on the tops of the toes, with the heels well raised off the floor showing beautiful arches. It should not be interpreted like a reel – fast and furious or aggressive. On landing it should be silent and graceful, like a swan gliding through the water, body and neck at full stretch. A perfect slip jig for me includes rocks, especially long rocks, with variations of front, back, side rocks, double, long and slow. The slip jig is an ideal dance to incorporate the 'rock' movement, which is considered to be very traditional in Irish dance.

For a pure and graceful performance of a slip jig refer to Michael Flatley's Lord of The Dance and the character Saoirse's performance of Celtic Dreams, and the ensemble performing with her. Another memorable interpretation is in Michael's Celtic Tiger, the number called 'The Garden of Eden'.

Basic/Beginner Slip Jig 9/8 Time

The starting position is as in a basic reel.

The Lead Around

The right foot is pointed in front. Bend the right knee and raise the foot to the level of the back knee, and hop twice on the left foot. Now put the right foot down in front of the left foot with a little jump,

Light shoe ensemble with Bernadette Flynn in Lord of the Dance.

'Stolen Kiss' by Bernadette Flynn in Lord of the Dance.

landing on the toes, and bring the left foot forwards as you land. Repeat the same movement with the left foot, and then repeat with the right foot. Count hop, hop, down right foot; hop, hop, down left foot; hop, hop, down right foot.

Now the right foot is down in front, weight bearing, bring the left foot to the front, level with the back knee, hop on the right foot and do a jump two three (as in the jump two three in the basic reel – the word-ing is hop and jump two three); this takes four bars. Now repeat the four bars on the right foot to the starting position, making a total of eight bars.

Basic Sidestep for a Beginner Slip Jig

Place the right foot in front with the toe pointed, with the weight on the back left foot. Take a step to the right with the right foot, and follow behind with the left foot sliding/dragging up to the heel of the right foot. Then take two steps, keeping the right foot in front for two, three (right, left). It is counted as a step and slide two, three. Repeat this twice more: with the right foot still in front, raise the right foot to the back knee while hopping with the left foot, followed by jump two, three, as in the end of the lead around.

The count goes as follows: step and slide two, three; step and slide two, three; step and slide two, three; hop and jump two, three (remember on the jump to switch legs). The left foot is now in front, and repeat going to the left with the left foot in front: this takes eight bars to complete.

Basic First Step for a Beginner Slip Jig

For the first step, place the right toe behind the left foot: now bring the right foot forwards and put the heel of the right foot down in front; now jump with both feet together on the toes; then dance hop and jump two, three as above. Repeat with the left foot, then twice more to complete eight bars.

For the slow walk-through, take the right foot behind the left, putting the toe of the right foot down behind for count one; now bring the right foot to the front, putting the heel down for count two; keep the right foot in front and do a jump with both feet for count three. Now raise the right foot up in front to the back knee, and perform a hop jump two, three. As mentioned above, perform this four times with the right foot, left foot, right foot, left foot: this counts as the first step.

As in the previous beginner dances, another eight bars may be performed, consisting of similar steps as in the lead around, the sidestep and the first step. Emphasize the slip jig count of one, two, three, four, five, also hop and jump two threes, keeping well up on the toes of both feet and with the heels up off the floor throughout.

The Treble Jig

The next solo dance to learn is the treble jig: as the light jig, it is also a double jig in 6/8 time, but played more slowly. It is danced in heavy shoes, and is usually the first heavy shoe dance that is learnt. Treble is the basic movement; it is also known as a

Old- and new-style hard shoes suitable for treble jig hornpipe and set dances.

shuffle, a rally, or a batter. It is similar to a shuffle in tap dance.

Standing with the right foot in front, lift the right foot slightly with the weight on the back foot, brush the right foot outwards in a small sweeping/brushing movement, making a tap sound as you brush and hit the floor. Keep it low to the floor and now bring it inwards to you in a similar brush movement. These are both short, loose strokes. Here are some examples of counting and drilling the movement – it is very important to get the count time and rhythm correct.

Drills for the Treble Jig

1. With the right foot in front:
   Out, in (that is, brush out and brush in), twice = one bar
   Repeat: out, in; out, in = one bar
   Repeat: out, in; out, in = one bar
   Repeat: out, in; out, in = one bar
   This makes a total of four bars.

Now do the same with the left foot in front, making a total of four bars.

2. This is the same movement, but saying it musically:
   DA: DA: out, in (brush out, brush in), twice = one bar
   DA: DA: + DA: DA = one bar
   DA: DA: + DA: DA = one bar
   DA: DA: + DA: DA = one bar
   This makes a total of four bars.

Learning to treble/brush out.

Learning to treble/brush in.

Now change feet and do the same with the left foot, making a total of four bars.

It is important when learning and drilling this movement that the foot, especially the ankles, is kept very loose and flexible. As you can see, each out, in movement is a half bar of 6/8 music, so doing it twice equals one bar. Understanding this helps to fit it correctly to music. When drilling with music, keep alternating the feet after four or eight bars of music to gain equal strength of rhythm on both the right and the left feet.

The Lead Around

This is a heavy jig step suitable for a lead around for a beginner heavy shoe jig. The starting position is the right foot in front, and as in the first bar in the light jig dance, perform the same piece, leading with the right foot dance, up, back hop one, two, three (refer to the first bar of the lead around of the light jig). Now do a skip hop one, two, three with the left foot, and repeat the same skip one, two, three with the right foot. Now do four single trebles (shuffles): left foot,

right foot, left foot, right foot, and (now finish with a double treble on the left foot) treble, treble hop back, hop back two, three, four. This makes eight bars of music. Repeat again for another eight bars on the right foot again, to complete the circle.

Counting is up, back, hop one, two, three; skip one, two, three; skip one, two, three; treble one, treble two, treble three, treble four, treble, treble hop back, hop back two three four. This makes sixteen bars of music for a full lead around, usually in a clockwise direction.

Now dance the sidestep, as explained below. Then add a further eight bars on the right foot, repeated on the left foot, with combined movements of the lead around and sidestep, adding skips, hops and heel movement, especially using the single and double treble rhythms.

Sidestep

Place the right foot in front, with the weight on the back foot. Starting with the right foot, dance three trebles, alternating the feet and your weight – that is, right foot, left foot, right foot (count treble one, treble two, treble three – the weight is now on the back foot). Keep the right foot in front for a count of one, two, three, four beats – that is, front back, front back: with the right foot still in front, now do a double treble with the right foot, bringing it back behind the left foot with a hop – and now dance hop back two, three, four with the left foot, bringing it back behind the right foot for the count of one, two, three, four, which equals eight bars. (The last two bars are similar to the last two bars of the lead around.)

Now do exactly the same, starting with the left foot, which equals eight bars.

Practise the sidestep with the right and the left foot, which equals eight bars, with music.

First Step

The first step will be danced on the right foot for eight bars, and then repeated on the left foot for a further eight bars. The step is exactly the same, or similar in content, to either the first step of St Patrick's Day or the middle step of St Patrick's Day both in time and content.

The Hornpipe

The second dance in heavy shoe to progress to is 'the hornpipe'. The hornpipe is in metronomic speed 144, 4/4 time signature and is danced in heavy shoe. The beginner hornpipe is played faster than the open advanced hornpipe, which is danced in championships and at advanced level. The slower version allows the dancer to include more intricacies in footwork and more syncopation in the steps to be performed.

It is important for a dancer, when learning the hornpipe, to learn and understand the difference in rhythm between a hornpipe and a jig, and to be able to dance one bar of each, tapping it and dancing it out in its correct rhythm. A double treble in jig time 6/8 is a totally different rhythm to a double treble in hornpipe time 4/4 – it's faster in jig time and is longer and slower in hornpipe.

A double treble in jig time is counted treble, treble hop back, which as explained above equals one bar, whereas in the hornpipe you do one brush (more like a tip) and put it down in front with a little jump

or spring, and switch feet, bringing the next foot forwards. Do the same with this foot now in front, tip, put it down in front, switch like before, and with the first foot now in front treble hop back, bring it back and put weight on it behind. Count the bar like this – starting with the right foot, tip and tip and treble hop back equals one bar of hornpipe music. Continue in the same manner going from foot to foot until eight are completed, equal to eight bars.

A Basic Lead Up for a Beginner Hornpipe

In the hornpipe the first sixteen bars are usually referred to as a lead up or lead out, comprising eight bars on the right foot, repeated on the left foot, making a total of sixteen bars. Proceed as follows:

- Adopt the starting position with the right foot in front. With the weight on the left foot behind, tip with the right foot and put down in front, tip with the left foot, place down in front of you – now

Executing blocks in hornpipe.

the right front is in front treble and put it down in front, counting one, two, one, two. Finish with the weight on the left foot behind: this equals bar one.

- Now tip again with the right foot and switch to the left foot treble, and repeat one, two, one, two (keeping the left in front): this equals bar two.
- Keep doing tip and tip, treble one, two, one, two, alternating the feet, twice more: this equals bar three and bar four.
- The left foot is now in front and the weight is on the right foot behind: step down on the left foot, transferring the weight, and bring the right foot forwards and treble and hop back. Put the right foot down behind now and transfer the weight on to it: this equals bar five.
- Now tip with the left, tip with the right and treble hop back with the left: this equals bar six.
- Now tip with the right, tip with the left, and treble hop back with the right: this equals bar seven.
- Now step down on the left foot in front and treble hop, keeping the right foot in front; hop again with

the left foot and treble again with the right foot and bring it behind: this equals bar eight.

Now practise the above full eight bars on the right foot:

- tip and tip treble one, two, one, two (bar one)
- tip treble one, two, one, two (bar two)
- tip treble one, two, one, two (bar three)
- tip treble one, two, one, two (bar four)
- down treble hop back (bar five)
- tip and tip treble hop back (bar six)
- tip and tip treble hop back (bar seven)
- down treble hop and treble hop back (bar eight)

The hornpipe step is referred to as the first step – it is not usual to dance a sidestep in a hornpipe. The step would be of a similar beat and rhythm as the lead up. This is about the number of bars danced in a beginner hornpipe. Advanced hornpipes are usually forty bars with the music slower to allow for intricacies of syncopation.

PART TWO: OTHER SOLO TRADITIONAL DANCE MOVEMENTS AND SET DANCES

REVIEW

All the light shoe basic dances are now completed – easy reel, light jig single jig and slip jig – also the heavy shoe dances such as the treble jig and the hornpipe; now we can move on to a more advanced grade in these dances, especially in the reel and slip jig. The timing and time signature will be the same, but the music will be played slightly more slowly to enable more intricate footwork to be incorporated into the routines.

Other movements such as rocks, cross keys and boxes (boxes are more common in heavy shoe) can be learnt and introduced into your dancing. These are very traditional movements and are found in traditional set dances; they will be described later in this chapter. Their popularity never dies, and

teachers and choreographers still use them in the most advanced and up-to-date modern material in both light and heavy shoe. The creative minds of these people have no limits, the bar gets higher all the time, and they have brought a native tradition to a beautiful art form, which is performed worldwide.

TRADITIONAL DANCE MOVEMENTS

The Rocks

The next dance core movement to learn is known as the rocks. Rocks have various forms and lengths, and are usually danced in three counts. They include front rocks, a basic back rock and a long rock (about five counts). They can be combined, or a long slow rock can be extended into a faster beat, or vice versa. You can go from front rock to back, changing feet and not forgetting the side rock – the combinations are limitless. They can be performed in light shoe or heavy shoe.

The Basic Rock

Let's start in light shoe with the basic rock. First learn the fundamentals: stand in front of a full-length mirror as this is the best way to learn, practise and drill, day after day until you have mastered it. It is helpful, especially when learning the position and gaining your balance, to use two strong chairs, with firm backs, about the height of your elbows. Put the backs of the chairs facing each other in front of the mirror. Now in light shoes stand between the two chairs with each hand resting on a chair back: when you stand up on your toes and with your hands pressing into the chair, your arms should be able to take your weight. Hold your balance, so the chairs are taking your weight. This way you can move slowly from side to side, and even stop or pause in between.

With the right foot in front of the left, stand on the toes of both feet; then raising the right foot and with the weight on the back foot, hop on the back foot and bring the right foot behind, putting it down on the outside of the left foot. The weight is now on both feet, still on the toes of both feet: so that was hop back and down on the outside right leg, one count.

Now lock the legs together from the feet up to the top of the legs, closing from the ankles up, the same at the knees and the same with the thighs. Look in the mirror to check that there is no space: you should not be able to see through at any place all the way up – this is called locking. Keeping locked, sway to your left, staying on your toes, then keeping all locked, sway to your right for the second count, then sway again to the left for the third count. Try that again: hop, rock two, three, allowing the chairs to take your weight and balance. This is the basic rock.

Then try it with the other foot. Keep it going for eight bars of reel music, alternating the feet, with a hop starting each one. As you get more proficient you can step away from the chairs and

try keeping you own balance, with a nice swaying, locked movement.

This can be developed into the many variations mentioned above – you can do the front rock by stepping to the side, but keep the foot in front – if it's the right foot, step to the right and lock the left foot behind on the outside of the right and sway right, left, right, and so on. Now try a long rock with two slow and three quick, slow, slow, quick, quick, quick. You can devise many variations also changing feet – the choices are endless.

Learning to rock in light shoe supported by two chairs: 1. The legs and feet completely locked, then sway to the right – **count one.**

2. Maintaining the locked position, sway to the left – **count two.**

3. Still in the locked position, well up on the toes and the heels off the floor, finish straight up – **count three**.

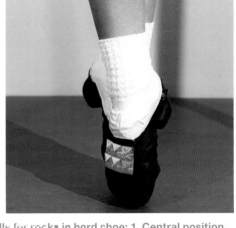

Drills for rocks in hard shoe: 1. Central position.

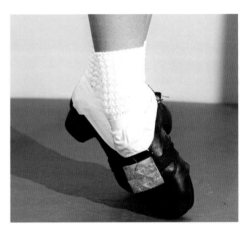

Rocks in hard shoe: 2. Rock to the right.

Performing the sequence in light shoe without a chair.

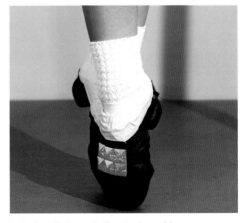

Rocks in hard shoe: 3. Central position.

Rocks in hard shoe: 4. Rock to the left.

Rocks in hard shoe: 5. Central position.

Side Rocks

Now try a similar movement called a side rock. Stand with the feet side by side and on the toes. Keep the weight on both feet, keeping the toes on the floor, and swivel on the toes from side to side, usually for a count of three. Lock in the same manner as for the rocks above, with the ankles, knees and the tops of the legs closed and pulled tight; keep high on the toes with a good arch.

The Cross Keys

Another traditional movement that is still very popular in present-day Irish dancing is the cross key. It is a very distinctive movement and needs to be executed specifically. Like a rock, a back cross key can be done or a front one. It can be performed in light shoe or heavy shoe. The light shoe version will be demonstrated here as it is easier to manipulate the feet one around the other, but the moves and elements are the same in both.

You may also find the use of the chairs a help to start with. Place the chairs in the same position as for the rock, or easier still, sit on a chair looking into a mirror: in this way you are taking the weight and balance off your body, but your feet are learning the movement. Let's take it from the standing position, so you know when and where to transfer the weight.

There are various ways of describing this movement, each having their own interpretation and count but achieving the same result. I will go through my interpretation and count. Stand in front of the mirror, with the right foot in the starting position in front, and call this the leading foot. Pull up on the toes of both feet weight bearing, not lifting either foot off the floor; turn or twist both feet inwards and the heels outwards. Now drop back on the heels bearing weight, and turning or twisting them (the heels) inwards, and bring them together. Lift the leading foot (the right), put the weight on the left for a moment, then bring the right behind and step down on it.

As the right foot is going back your weight is on the left heel: do a turn on it, sliding it in front as the right does the step back and down behind. That last bit of leaning on the heel is the 'key' movement, and is most important to finishing the movement correctly; the last piece of the movement on the heel is called 'turning the key'. Many a point has been lost by a

Drills for cross keys in four moves: 1. Central position with the right foot in front.

Cross keys: 2. Push the heels out and the toes in.

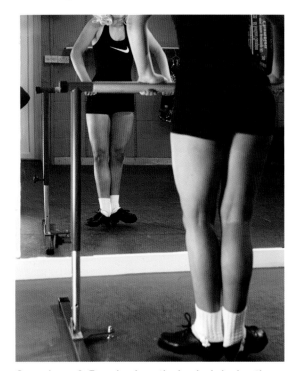

Cross keys: 3. Drop back on the heels, bringing them together with the toes flexed.

Cross keys: 4. Remain on the left heel bearing weight, bringing the right foot behind the left heel: this twists out and in, finishing with the right foot behind.

competitor not turning the key and completing the movement.

So broken down slowly: up on the toes with the weight on both feet, turn (twist) both feet inwards for *one*. Drop down on the heels and slide them inwards, closing the heels in (and the toes outwards), with the weight on the heels for *two*. Continue with the weight on the left heel, bring the right foot behind, put it down, turning/twisting on the left heel for *three*. This can be performed on either foot; whichever foot starts in front will finish behind.

Boxes

Like the rock and cross keys, the box is a very traditional movement and can be found in the traditional set dances; like the other movement it is still very popular, especially in the heavy shoe. In a similar manner there are many variations, from a single box into doubling and tripling in a syncopated manner. In the single traditional manner these must also be executed and completed correctly, and to do this the movement must finish by 'closing the box' – that is, when on both heels bring the toes inwards to meet and tip together.

Basically, step on one heel, and place the other heel beside it: with the feet now side by side and the weight on both heels, turn them out with the toes pointing out and flexed. Then without raising them off the floor, turn them inwards for the toes to tip together, so they go out and in, then step back on to the ball of one foot, putting it down behind. In traditional sets it can be performed to a count of four or five.

Clicks

Clicks are an elevated movement, when at one point both feet meet or pass each other as high in the air as possible and hit off each other making a clicking sound. It is every dancer's dream to execute beautifully elevated clicks, no matter which form: front or long click, side click, leaps, or up and overs, birds, or back clicks. The more athletic and the fitter you are, the more adventurous you can be and develop them into doubles and triples.

Drills for boxes: **Count one:** Bring the right heel forwards bearing weight, the toes flexed.

Drills for boxes: **Count two:** Bring the left heel alongside the right, with the weight now on both heels and the toes still flexed, and swivel the toes outwards.

Drills for boxes: **Count three:** While still on the heels, bring the toes inwards to tip and close the box.

Drills for boxes: **Count four:** Step back with the left foot.

Let's look at the single movement first. The following points apply to whichever variation you propose to do:

- Never drop the heels, either taking off or on landing (so you need a strong arch to hold you up).
- Land lightly on the toes with no sound (except when in heavy shoe when you will hear a click sound, although there should be no sound from the other foot or a drop heel sound).
- Your posture (carriage) must remain upright with no bend of the body or movement of the arms, either while taking off, while suspended or when landing.
- Both legs, but especially your lead or working leg, should remain very straight, especially when you are airborne (elevated), *with no bend at the knee*.

When executing any of these movements, the toes must be pointed and the feet arched – do not show the sole of the foot.

Front or Long Clicks

The second or follow-through leg should be just as straight as the lead leg. It should land in the same manner, silently, straight, the knee pulled and heel up. The most important sound is that of the heels clicking off each other as they pass (if in light shoe it will be just a light sound). Points can be gained or lost here. All the above points apply to double and triple clicks.

Side Clicks

There are variations of side click, which can be done with straight legs or legs bent at the knee. When doing it with straight legs, if the lead/working leg is the right leg, elevate it to the right side so it is fully extended and straight, then bring the second leg up to meet it so they join together side by side (suspended), connecting at a right angle. To finish the movement the lead leg usually continues on up after connecting, still dead straight, as the second leg lands, followed by the lead leg. This usually takes one bar of music. The side click can be done with the knees bent to the side in similar fashion, but without continuing up at the end.

Leaps or Up and Overs

This is a very versatile movement. It is equally effective in both light and heavy shoe reel for boys and girls, and can be very graceful and elegant in a girl's slip jig, especially if she floats through the air. It is also a very popular hard shoe movement, especially when the dancer has the ability to hold and pause in the air (but keeping it in the same time frame otherwise it becomes a Bird). The lead leg should be totally straight and firm, and the second leg tucked right up under the bottom. Other variations include following through with the second leg passing the lead leg to the front in a kick-out motion, or going into the initial leap with a leg bent at the knee and follow-through.

To get good elevation in this movement, especially with the first variation, it is essential to take a lead or step with the secondary foot pushing off the ground (as long as you do *not* drop your heel in take-off); this can give a good spring to your elevation and gain extra height. *The golden rule on landing is not to drop the heels.* The arches need to be strong, so do plenty of exercises for this.

The Bird

This is not a traditional movement, though it must be said that the versions of the clicks above are today's style of execution. The Bird came into being in the 1970s. It sometimes goes by other names, but The Bird describes it best. I and a group of dancers were performing at a concert in Dublin. After rehearsals, a group of us remained on stage filling in time and doing a few steps. I suggested they simulated taking flight like a bird, jumping through the air with the lead leg straight and the other tucked up under their bottom tightly, then brush with the lead leg going straight up on the first hop, with the back foot still squeezed and pointed underneath. That was the birth of The Bird, in this format.

The Butterfly

The Butterfly is another cross-key movement. It is based on a cross key in the air, with both feet elevated, but the same principles apply. Bring the lead foot behind, tuck it under the other foot (a little

Bird in flight.

towards the outside), push off the floor with a jump with both feet, and flick the feet (toes) outwards and the heels inwards connecting. While still elevated, bring the front foot behind and land on the floor on both feet, staying on the toes (do not drop the heels).

To perfect foot movement and placement without putting strain on carriage, sit on a chair and keep drilling the movement till it is smooth and the feet know what they are doing. Then stand between the two chairs, with the chair backs facing each other, in the same way as suggested in the rock movement. Facing the mirror, put the hands and weight on the top of the chair backs. These are now supporting you and taking your weight, again in the same way as for the rock; land on both feet, up on toes, or high on ball of foot.

When you have mastered this and can take your own weight, set aside the chairs and keep drilling in front of the mirror, perfecting the execution of the movement. Finish with the feet crossed – the foot you lead with usually finishes at the back.

Summary

We have now completed the beginner/basic dances, the reel, light jig, single jig (hop jig) and slip jig, which are the four light shoe dances, and the beginner/basic heavy shoe dances, the treble jig and the hornpipe, and some additional movements. We have also learnt how to practise, drill and execute them, which is crucial for composing and choreographing steps and dances. We have also learnt some

Butterfly: 1. Sit on a chair with the feet raised off the floor, the right foot in front of the left, with both feet pointing downwards.

Butterfly: 2. Push the heels outwards.

Butterfly: 3. Flick the toes outwards and bring the heels together.

Butterfly: 4. Bring the right foot to the back and land with the weight on both feet up on the toes.

traditional and innovative movements. It is now time to turn to set dances.

TRADITIONAL SET DANCES

Traditional set dances are performed in heavy shoes and are in either jig or hornpipe tempo, and are danced at a similar speed to the basic treble jig and hornpipe, which is a faster speed than the modern set dance. There are two parts to these dances: the step and the set. The first part is usually shorter than the second. The first part is called 'the lead up' and is danced on the right foot, then repeated on the left foot; the second part, the set, is nowadays usually just performed on the right foot. There was a time when not only the left foot set was danced, but then the first part step was danced again, and possibly a second set and a last step. In order to standardize and preserve the dances it was decided to dance the lead up on the right and the left foot, and the set on the right foot.

These dances have been handed down through the ages, and most of the dance organizations make a great effort to preserve them as near as possible to their original choreography and origin. Apart from having some regional variations, the sentiment is to preserve them as closely as possible to their original invention and interpretation.

They must be danced in a traditional manner: there is no room for any modernization or embellishments.

Traditional movements such as rocks, cross keys and boxes must be performed and executed correctly, with no short cuts. Neither can movements such as clicks be added.

As written in the CLRG website[8]: 'Dancers are not permitted to move in a counter direction when executing "rolls".' Rolls may be danced on the spot or moving in the direction of the leading foot: for example, the first bar of music in King of the Fairies may be danced on the spot or to the right when on the right foot, or on the spot or moving to the left when on the left foot. Rocks in any traditional set dance must be fully completed and not cut short. In Job of Journeywork, boxes may be executed in either four or five beats. The box must be completed by the two shoes touching at the toe piece. There is no stamp immediately following the box.

There are seven traditional set dances on the CLRG list. Those considering competitive dancing in grade competitions, or taking grade or teacher exams, need to know all these traditional set dances.[19]

TRADITIONAL SET DANCES AS LISTED BY CLRG

NAME	TIME
St Patrick's Day	6/8 Jig time
Jockey to the Fair	6/8 Jig time
Three Sea Captains	6/8 Jig time
Job of Journeywork	4/4 Hornpipe time
Garden of Daisies	4/4 Hornpipe time
The Blackbird	2/4 Hornpipe time
The King of the Fairies	2/4 Hornpipe time

Visual demonstrations of these dances can be found on the websites of the various Irish dance organizations or on YouTube.

Set Dances

Solo set dances should not be confused with the social form of dance also known as set dances, where a full set is made up of four couples and a half set of two couples. They were brought in from France, England and Scotland, and derived from quadrilles and English country dances. They were adapted and taught by the travelling dancing masters across Ireland from the late eighteenth and early nineteenth centuries. Conradh na Gaeilge – The Gaelic League – established in 1893, banned set dancing, and further developed and promoted ceílí dancing. In the 1970s Comhaltas Ceoltóirí Éireann and some other organizations supported the revival of set dancing.

Solo Set Dances

The set dance in this context is a hard shoe solo dance, danced to a particular tune that is in two parts, A and B: this is explained in more detail below.

As pupils progress up through the grades system, they move on to more complicated forms of the reel, slip jig, single jig in light shoe and the treble jig and hornpipe in heavy shoe. When they are ready for championship level competition, they take a step further to what is known as the set dance.

This is usually performed in the third round of a championship, and the competitor has to be recalled for this particular round – usually comprising the top half or a given percentage of the competitors – especially at oireachtaisí, national and world championship events. These events are run by the various organizations in each region of each country, and then nationally. The regional event in CLRG is a qualifying round for their world championships. Each organization has their own specific list of set dances, and although there are a few variations in each, the majority are very similar. The CLRG list of forty is as follows:

In 2/4 hornpipe time: The Lodge Road, Rodney's Glory, The Blackbird, Planxty Davis, King of the Fairies and The Downfall of Paris. The minimum speed for all of these is seventy-six.

In 4/4 hornpipe time: Ace and Deuce of Pipering, Youghal Harbour, Bonapartes Retreat, The Hunt, Garden of Daisies, Job of Journeywork, Madam Bonaparte, The Piper, Kilkenny Races, The Rambling Rake, The White Blanket, The Blue-Eyed Rascal, The Roving Pedlar and The Four Masters. The minimum speed for all is seventy-six.

In 6/8 jig time: The Three Sea Captains, The Hurling Boys, Rub The Bag, Hurry The Jug, The Funny Tailor (Drunken Gauger), The Blackthorn Stick, St Patrick's Day, Jockey to the Fair, Planxty Drury, Humours of Bandon, The Orange Rogue, Miss Brown's Fancy, Planxty Hugh O'Donnell, The Storyteller, The Fiddler around the Fairy Tree, The Sprig of Shillelagh, The Wandering Musician, The Vanishing Lake, The Charlady. The minimum speed for all 6/8 time set dances is sixty-six.

6/8+9/8, jig and slip jig time: Is The Big Man Within. The minimum speed is sixty-six.

These sets are comprised of two parts: the first part A, referred to as 'the step', is danced on the right foot and repeated on the left foot. The second part B, referred to as 'the set', is danced on the right foot only. Part A is usually longer than part B, and the bars in both A and B vary for each dance.

The choreography – which is usually done by the teacher, and sometimes older senior dancers do their own – is very important, and the music, the time signature, the rise and fall of the music, and light and shade should be interpreted carefully. The recall for the set dance is the highlight of the competition, and whereas the earlier solo rounds are danced in twos or threes on the stage together, the set dance is danced with each dancer performing on their own, so the rhythm and interpretation is seen, heard and fully appreciated. Delivery of good timing and execution is key, notwithstanding carriage, of course. Most of the set dances have a story behind them or the name of the dance has a relevance. This should be interpreted in the choreography, along with the rise and fall of the music, as mentioned above.

Ella Owens performing at a world championship.

There is a minimum speed for both hornpipe and jig sets, below which the dancer cannot go. The main difference here is in the hornpipe sets, where the dancer can take either the faster speeds, which are closer to the regular hornpipe time – popular speeds are between 107 up to 112, or higher – or the slower minimum speed of 76. The problem here is, in taking it down to 76 it is turned more into jig time than hornpipe time,

EXAMPLES OF SOLO SET DANCES

2/4 hornpipe time	The Lodge Road	Part A = 8 bars	Part B = 20 bars
2/4 time	Planxty Davis	Part A = 16 bars	Part B = 16 bars
4/4 hornpipe time	Kilkenny Races	Part A = 8 bars	Part B = 24 bars
4/4 hornpipe time	Youghal Harbour	Part A = 6 bars	Part B = 14 bars
6/8 jig time	Planxty Drury	Part A = 12 bars	Part B = 16 bars
6/8 jig time	The Vanishing Lake	Part A = 14 bars	Part B = 18 bars

and there is a school of thought that believes this should not be done.

However, it is allowable for a dancer to take the speed 76 in hornpipe time. To do this they need to be in top class physical condition, very aerobically fit, and their timing and rhythm needs to be impeccable. It is a very demanding, high-impact workout. The choreography should not be laborious or overloaded, but rather should flow with the rhythm and fit in effortlessly. The choreography of these set pieces is a highly skilled craft and a gift in itself. Many excellent teachers bring choreographers who are talented in this field, into their class to do this specifically. The creative side, as in choreography, is not everyone's forte, much as was the case with the travelling dance masters in the eighteenth and nineteenth centuries. The tradition lives on.

Interpreting a Story or Dance Name

This section on set solo dances describes how musicians and choreographers interpret a story or the name of the dance through the music and choreography. In 2011 The Marie Duffy Foundation set up and funded two competitions, one for entrepreneurial musicians to compose a new piece of

Ella Owens preparing to dance The Vanishing Lake.

music suitable for a solo set dance, and the second for dancers to choreograph a new set dance to the winning tune. For the first competition eleven entries were submitted; the winning composition was The Vanishing Lake, composed by Francis Ward, with The Charlady, composed by Michael Fitzpatrick, a close second. Both of these compositions have now been added to the CLRG official list of set dances and are used regularly at feiseanna and major competitions worldwide.

The competition for the Irish dance choreography to the winning composition was held in Dublin in February 2012. Again, eleven entries were submitted, and the winning routine was danced by Cathal Keany.

Both stories are related below, and how the composers translated them into the music for a new set dance.

The Vanishing Lake
The Story

Lougareema, or the Vanishing Lake as it is known, lies not far from Ballycastle, Co. Antrim, at the north-east tip of Ireland. It seems to disappear and reappear at random. The road to Ballycastle runs right through the lake, but does not sit high enough to avoid flooding.

Towards the end of the 1800s, a certain Colonel John Magee McNeille wanted to get to Ballycastle after having spent a few days with his cousin, Captain Daniel McNeille. Anxious to catch the 3pm train from the town, McNeille persuaded a coachman to drive him in a covered wagon pulled by two horses. The road disappeared into the waters of the flooded lake as the wagon neared it, but he coaxed the coachman to try to pass. Half-way across the horses began to get nervous as the freezing cold water reached their bellies. At first they were obedient and kept going, but soon fright overtook them.

Impatient to get to the station, McNeille took the whip to one of the beasts: it responded by rearing up on its back legs and turned to the side, slipping off the road into the deeper waters. The other horse had no choice but to follow, and the carriage soon ended up submerged in deep water. McNeille struck out for where he knew the higher land of the road to be. But weighed down by his heavy winter clothes and with the struggling horses flailing wildly about between him and safety, the Colonel succumbed to the treacherous cold waters. He was buried a few days later not far away, in Ramoan churchyard.[20]

The Music Composition
The above story is typical of the traditional tales behind most set dances. Francis Ward has created a piece of music that truly reflects the sadness of the story, and his thinking behind his haunting but beautiful composition is highlighted below.

Musical description:	Key: A minor
Time signature:	6/8 jig
Bars in step part A:	14
Bars in set part B:	18
Total number of bars	46

In composing the set dance Francis considered three main factors:

• That the tune when performed at dance competition tempos was suitable for dancing in terms of strong dance rhythm and phrasing.
• That the length was sufficiently long to showcase the prowess of a championship dancer. He believes there are many long hornpipe set dances, but in terms of long jig set dances it is usually the 'big two', Drunken Gauger and Blackthorn Stick, that are performed, and occasionally Planxty Drury and Three Sea Captains. Therefore, when composing this set dance, he decided to offer championship dancers and their teachers an alternative to these jig set dances. Thus, the composition is in jig time and comparable in length to the commonly danced jig sets.
• Variation of key: Drunken Gauger, Blackthorn Stick, Planxty Drury and Three Sea Captains are all in major (happy) keys, so Francis composed his piece in a minor key, again to offer another variation for dancers, teachers, musicians and listeners alike.

Finally, Francis notes that the structure of set dances performed at Irish dance competitions are AAAB, as follows: A – introduction played; AA – step part danced on the right foot, repeated on the left foot; B – the set part performed on the right foot only. The set dance is recorded with the structure AAABB – that is, the step part three times and the set part twice.[20]

The Charlady
The Story
In contrast to Francis' traditional story, Michael's The Charlady is a more contemporary story. Looking over the fields on a rainy afternoon Michael was piecing together the notes of his composition and at the same time trying to find a name that would complement the tune. As always, he began to think in terms of things that had been a unique or an integral part to the Irish experience – something that would pay tribute to an era – an event or even a person. Then one evening he thought of the charlady, a character from the past whose role was to do chores around the house – a term he had heard especially in Dublin. These ladies were always loyal

COMPOSITION OF SET DANCES

Name of the set dance	Key	Bars in step part	Bars in set part	Total number of bars dancing
Drunken Gauger	Major	15 × 2	15	45
Blackthorn Stick	Major	15 × 2	15	45
Three Sea Captains	Major	8 × 2	20	36
Planxty Drury	Major	12 × 2	14	38
The Vanishing Lake	Minor	14 × 2	18	46

to the family they worked for, and life was good for the children of those families because the charlady was always a reliable presence, always there with a kind word and a helping hand.[21]

The Music Composition

Musical description:	Key: A major
Time signature	6/8 jig
Bars in step part A	8
Bars in set part B:	24
Total number of bars	40

Michael's idea behind his composition was to create a set dance that might be a humble alternative to the beautiful and incredibly popular set dances used, namely Drunken Gauger, Blackthorn Stick, and of late Planxty Hugh O'Donnell, and that it would be long enough to showcase a dancer's skill and stamina. When danced in competition, Planxty Hugh O'Donnell is the longest jig set, measuring forty-eight bars, with Drunken Gauger and Blackthorn Stick being the

second longest with forty-five bars. The next longest jig set, at thirty-six bars, is the Three Sea Captains, but whilst also very popular, it is not anywhere near so as Drunken Gauger or Blackthorn Stick.

While Planxty Hugh O'Donnell is a relative newcomer to the official list of set dances, Michael believes it is now only starting to be seen at oireachtasí – but the earlier doubt that it is too long still remains. With all of these thoughts in mind, his plan was to write a set dance that would be forty bars in length when danced. To achieve the bar count an eight-bar A part and a twenty-four-bar B part, as noted in the very popular hornpipe set The Kilkenny Races, would become the desired bar-count infrastructure.[21]

NOTE: Budding choreographers, or those interested in following up the history, story or name of other and older set dances, might refer to the excellent book *Jigs to Jacobites* by Orfhlaith Ní Bhriain and Michael McCabe, in which 4,000 years of history are told through forty traditional set dances.[22]

A perfect line.

CHAPTER 5

CÉILÍ DANCING

They twirled and rocked, intertwined and separated, nearly leaning on to one another but barely touching, their movements sometimes tender sometimes almost violent... Moments passed while the dancers held tightly to each other as though their bodies were melting together. The expression on their features as they lifted their faces to the sky was one of unimaginable joy.

Hannah Fielding

This chapter will be split into the following three sections:

- What is a céilí? Definition and insight into the background and main elements of céilí dancing.
- *Ár Rincí Céilí*: the official CLRG céilí dance book. Thirty popular céilí dances by An Coimisiùn Le Rincí Gaelacha.[23]
- Céilí dances: a detailed description of, and dancing instructions for, ten of the most popular céilí dances.

WHAT IS A CÉILÍ?

A céilí (plural céilithe) is a traditional Irish or Scottish social gathering, where Irish or Scottish music, singing, traditional dancing and storytelling takes place. The dance masters taught sets and half sets in the nineteenth century, which derive from the quadrille and the French cotillion that were popular in France in the 1700s. They made their way to England and Ireland in the 1800s where they flourished, spreading to the houses and crossroads into the 1900s.

As stated earlier, Conradh na Gaeilge – the Gaelic League – was established in 1893 to promote the Irish language and all things cultural, including music, dancing and singing. In addition it wished to regain its political and cultural autonomy after being colonized for 800 years. Initially preserving the language was its primary aim, but then the league turned to other cultural aspects, such as dance. Sets were banished in favour of céilí dances. The first céilí was organized by the London branch of the Gaelic League and was held on 30 October 1897 in Bloomsbury, London. It is documented that sets of quadrilles and waltzes were also danced at this event.

The development of céilí dancing from the banning of set dancing and the Gaelic League spreading the teaching and learning of céilí dances as we know them today, is well covered in books on the history of Irish dancing. *Aspects of the History of Irish Dancing* and other works by Dr John Cullinane are very detailed and informative.[6]

A girls' céilí team in action.

OPPOSITE: **The start of a céilí team's career with Trip to the Cottage.**

Céilí dances differ from set dances in style and steps. In céilí dancing, dancers dance on their toes and the steps are simple and basic, consisting mainly of threes and sevens (see Chapter 4 for the basic solo dances and steps). There are also various forms of the rising step (see the section on competitive céilí dancing below).

Music and Instruments for Céilithe

The music used for these dances comprises various reels, jigs, single jigs and the hornpipe if The Three Tunes is included. The most popular instruments used by céilí bands are fiddles, flutes, piano and button accordions, pianos, bass, saxophone, bodhran drums, uilleann pipes, banjos and the double bass (as mentioned in the music section in Chapter 3).

Dance Terms

Similar to solo dancing, Irish céilí dancing has unique words that are used to describe various aspects of the dance and movements. The table below lists a number of terms frequently used throughout this guide that the beginner may not be familiar with, together with a brief explanation of their meaning.

ÁR RINCÍ CÉILÍ: THE OFFICIAL CLRG CÉILÍ DANCE BOOK

The official book of céilí dances issued by CLRG[23], *Ár Rincí Céilí*, describes thirty popular céilí dances. The next section gives the current list of these dances, which are used for all their examinations, grades and competitions, and are danced at céilithe. The list varies slightly in the different organizations, as do some of the rules and regulations. As CLRG is the largest of the global organizations, their system is described here.

For examination purposes candidates are expected to adhere to all the instructions, and have an in-depth knowledge of all thirty dances, from the set-up to the movements, music, the bars of music for each movement, the correct sequences, hand movements and footwork. An A to Z of each dance is laid out in the

World champions in the Senior Mixed Cóilí competition in the 1970s.

current edition of *Ár Rincí Céilí*. For the TCRG, and the TMRF teaching diplomas, the candidate needs to be able to teach groups of dancers any two of the thirty dances chosen at random. In addition, the written paper includes a two-hour written test on the candidate's knowledge of any of the thirty dances. For the SDCRG and ADCRG, the examiner and adjudicator examinations, a teaching test is not required, but an in depth two-hour written test is, together with some other elements, including interviews.

For céilí dancing in competition it is mandatory to follow all the rules and directions as given in the book. Embellishments are only allowed to ease the flow of the dance, and are scrutinized carefully by the adjudicator.

The Current Official List of the Thirty CLRG Céilí Dances

Ballaí Luimní/Walls of Limerick: A progressive dance in reel time, for any number of couples.

Cor Aontroma/Antrim Reel: A progressive dance in reel time, for any number of couples.

Briseadh na Carraige/Siege of Carrick: A progressive dance in jig time, for any number of couples. It is danced to the tune 'Haste to the Wedding'.

Réicí Mhala/Rakes of Mallow: A progressive dance in jig time, for any number of trios. The trios consist of a gentleman with two ladies on his right.

GLOSSARY OF CÉILÍ IRISH DANCING TERMS

Word	*Explanation*
Body	A group of movements that follows the opening movement and precedes the 'figures' of that particular dance. Each movement will have its own name, but overall it is referred to as the body.
Figure	Some dances have a first and second figure and some have more. They usually have an opening movement, the body, then the first figure. A figure is a specific movement, first performed by top couples, then sides (*see* below), to a specific number of bars. In most dances the body is danced between each figure and a finish.
Tops	The lead couple who performs the figures first.
Formation	Position of the dancers for either the opening or a specific movement.
Rise and grind	There are three variations: rise and grind, rising step, and sink and grind. It is performed in its various forms in 6/8 jig time.
Rising step	*See* above.
Sink and grind	*See* above.
Swing around	When a couple takes two hands together and swings around together in a clockwise direction.
Sides	The second couple to perform the figure movements.
Chain	A movement in which you take your partner's hands and continue taking alternate hands as you advance in an anticlockwise or clockwise direction, meeting other dancers in the set.
Promenade step	*See* Chapter 4, on solo dancing. It is the ordinary or skip threes.
The square	A movement in the Four Hands Reel and Fairy Reel.
Gates	A movement in the Gates of Derry – *see* specific description later in this chapter.
Telescope	A movement in the Gates of Derry – *see* specific description later in this chapter.
Quarters hook	A movement in Lannigan's Ball – *see* specific description later in this chapter.
Flirtation	A movement in Lannigan's Ball – *see* specific description later in this chapter.
Stack-up	A movement in Lannigan's Ball – *see* specific description later in this chapter.
See saw	A movement in The Three Tunes and The Sweets of May – *see* specific description later in this chapter.
Roly poly	A movement in The Three Tunes and The Sweets of May – *see* specific description later in this chapter.

Port an Fhómhair/Harvest Time Jig: A progressive dance in jig time, for any number of trios. The trios consist of a gentleman with a lady on either side of him.

Ionsaí na h Inse/Siege of Ennis: A progressive dance in jig time, in which each set of two couples is positioned in a line, facing another line of two couples.

Baint an Fhéir/Haymaker's Jig: A long dance in jig time for five couples in two lines, with the gentlemen in one line and the ladies in the other.

Droichead Átha Luain/The Bridge of Athlone: A progressive dance in jig and march time for any number of couples.

Tonnaí Thoraigh/Waves of Tory: A progressive dance in reel time for any number of couples positioned in two lines, with the gentlemen in one line and the ladies in the other.

Rince Fada/Long Dance: A progressive dance in jig time for any number of couples.

Deifir chun na Bainise/Haste to the Wedding: A progressive dance in jig time, danced to the tune of the same name, for any number of couples.

Bainise Uí Lonagáin/Lannigan's Ball: A round dance in single jig time, for six couples, danced to the tune of the same name. Adapted for competition to four couples.

An Rince Mór/Big Dance: A round dance in reel time for any number of couples.

Rince Mór na Tine/Bonfire Dance. A round dance in reel time for any number of couples.

Cor Ceathrar/Four-Hand Reel. A four-hand dance in reel time for two couples.

Pléarcha na Bandan/Humours of Bandon: A four-hand dance for two couples in jig time. Danced to the tune of the same name.

Cor Gleann Cearr/Glencar Reel: A six-hand dance in reel time for three couples, gentlemen on one side and ladies on the other.

Cór na Síog/Fairy Reel: A six-hand dance for two gentlemen and four ladies.

Cor an Diúic/Duke Reel: A six-hand dance in reel time for three couples.

Cor Ochtar/Eight-Hand Reel: An eight-hand dance in reel time for four couples.

Cor Muirgheis/Morris Reel: An eight-hand dance in reel time for four couples.

An Cor Casta/Cross Reel: An eight-hand dance in reel time for four couples.

Port Ochtar/Eight-Hand Jig: An eight-hand dance in jig time for four couples.

Lá Fhéile Phádraig/St Patrick's Day: An eight-hand dance in jig time, danced to the tune of the same name.

Turas 'an Tí/Trip to the Cottage: An eight-hand dance in jig time for four couples, danced to the tune of the same name.

Cadhp an Chúil Aird/High-Cauled Cap: An eight-hand dance in reel time. For four couples; it is danced to the tune of the same name.

Aoibhneas na Bealtaine/Sweets of May: An eight-hand jig in single jig. For four couples, danced to the tune of the same name.

Na Trí Foinn/The Three Tunes: An eight-hand dance for four couples. It is danced to three different tunes: 'Haste to the Wedding' (jig), 'Leslie's Hornpipe' and 'The German Beau' (reel).

Geataí Dhoire/Gates of Derry: An eight-hand dance in single jig time, for four couples. Danced to the tune 'The Quakers Wife'.

Cor Seisear Déag/Sixteen-Hand Reel: A sixteen-hand dance in reel time for eight couples.

Important Points to Remember

It is important to remember the following points, which in general are applicable to all the dances:

- The sidestep is the basis of all Irish dances, and needs to be mastered before the dances can be performed correctly.
- When the sidestep is not being danced, the simple (ordinary) one, two, three step either in reel time or jig time, 2/4 time or 6/8 time is danced (*see* the instruction on this in Chapter 4, the basic threes and sevens).
- Before attempting any particular dance, learn the above two steps and be able to move in every direction. Practise these steps to music, reels or jigs, dancing on the toes or the ball of the foot, with toes outwards and heels inwards, and the knees straight in front.
- Each movement is performed to a set number of bars in the music, so that when the dancers return to place at the completion of a movement, they are ready to commence the next.
- When partners are dancing round together, facing each other, the position of the arms (hands) is as follows: elbows bent, forearms bent upwards, ladies' hands crossed at the wrists, gentlemen's hands uncrossed, with the right hand in the right hand of the partner, and the left hand in the left, with the right hands above the left hands. Then holding the partners' hands uncrossed, when the gentlemen's hands are underneath the ladies' (except in Trip to the Cottage).

A starting formation for an eight-hand céilí.

Position of the arms and hands – note that the gentlemen's hands are underneath supporting the ladies'.

Position of the arms and hands – note the connecting hands in a chain movement.

- When partners are dancing beside each other, holding hands, the position of the arms is as follows: elbows bent, forearms bent upwards, the gentleman holding the partner's left hand in his right, with the gentleman's hand underneath the lady's.
- Always reflect the rhythm of the music in the movements of the feet. In sidestepping to the right always pass behind, in sidestepping to the left always pass in front.
- When dancing a swing around with a partner it is acceptable to use either the same foot or the opposite foot to the partner.
- Contrary couples are one and four, and couples two and three.
- Formation 'top of the room': in all four-hand, six-hand and eight-hand dances performed on stage, 'top of the room' refers to where the adjudicators are seated in front of the stage.
- In competition it is acceptable for teams to perform across stage in progressive dances.

The Rising Step

There are three versions of rising step in céilí dancing:

1. Rise and grind: danced with alternating feet (right and left foot).
2. Rising step: danced at the end of a sidestep or in cases where it is only danced once.
3. Sink and grind: danced twice on the right foot (the same foot).

It is danced in 6/8 time; the foot movements are described on the next page.

Foot movements for versions 1 & 2, rise and grind and rising step:

A. Hop on the left foot while raising the right foot in front with the toe pointed.
B. Hop again on the left foot while bringing the right foot to the back.
C. Place the right foot behind the left foot, transferring weight to it.
D. Hop on the right foot while bringing the left foot behind.
E. Place the left foot behind the right whilst raising the right foot.
F. Place the right foot down again.
G. Repeat E.
H. Repeat F.
   Also in 6/8 time.

Note: Emphasize the last four beats – hop back two, three, four.

To help you get the rhythm for these two versions, try dancing and counting as follows: hop, hop back, hop back two, three, four – and if repeating on the other leg, dance again: hop, hop back, hop back two, three, four.

Foot movements for version 3, sink and grind:

A. Jump on both feet together, the right foot in front of the left.
B. Hop on the left foot, raising the right foot in front.
C. Hop on the left foot, bringing the right foot behind.
D. Place the right foot behind the left while lifting a little off the ground.
E. Transfer the weight to the left foot.
F. Repeat D.
G. Repeat E.

Note: Emphasize the last four beats – hop back two, three, four.

Now try dancing and counting it as follows, which will help you get the rhythm: jump, hop, hop back, two, three, four, repeat jump, hop, hop back, two, three, four.

CÉILÍ DANCES

This section will look at some of the céilí dances that are popular both at céilíthe and in competitions. It will define what kind of dance it is, describe the set-up, give diagrammatic representations, and indicate the music used. It will start with the Walls of Limerick, which is the easiest for line-up, movements and steps.

Ballaí Luimní: Walls of Limerick

This is a progressive dance in reel time for any number of couples. Dancers line up in couples with the lady on the gentleman's right, the gentleman taking her left hand in his right, with his hand underneath hers. Each set consists of two couples facing each other. This is the simplest of all dances from the point of view of execution, always danced and a favourite at céilíthe.

Formation
The initial line-up is shown in the sketch and the photographs.

Gents X	
Ladies O	OX 8
	XO 7
	OX 6
	XO 5
	OX 4
	XO 3
	OX 2
	XO 1
	TOP OF ROOM.

Walls of Limerick starting formation.

Walls of Limerick Movements
Advance and retire: Partners take the inside hands, the gentleman's underneath the lady's. With the promenade step (basic threes), both couples advance towards each other (two bars), then retire to place (two bars). They then repeat the movement (four bars, making a total of eight bars).

Start of Walls of Limerick: the take-up position.

Walls of Limerick: the opening position with the hands.

Half right and left: Ladies exchange places with a sidestep on the left foot, passing each other face to face (two bars) finishing with two threes, while the gentlemen dance threes in place (four bars). The gentlemen now exchange places with a sidestep on the right foot, while the ladies dance threes in place (four bars, making a total of eight bars).

Dance with opposite: Each gentleman takes the right hand of the opposite lady and sidesteps to his left, finishing with two threes (four bars). All sidestep

back to place, finishing as before (four bars, making a total of eight bars).

Swing around: Already in a new position (on the opposite side of the set), partners face each other, and take both hands crossed (check notes to remember on taking hands). Each odd and even couple of the set swings around each other in an anticlockwise direction, revolving clockwise back to the new position, thus making a full circle. All finish facing in the same direction as at the start. (This makes a total of eight bars.)

Note: Couple no. 1 now faces couple no. 4, while couple no. 3 faces couple no. 6, and so on. Each even couple when reaching the top, and each odd couple when reaching the bottom of the line, stands idle during one complete round of the dance, and then recommences when the next couple moves on to meet them.

The couple at the top of the set are the leading couple, and the couple at the bottom of the set are the non-leading couple. The movements are repeated with each succeeding couple until the music ceases. In this manner, each couple progresses up or down the hall, with the result that couples dancing opposite each other are constantly varying, and for the duration are meeting new people.

Port an Fhómhair: The Harvest Time Jig

This is another progressive dance, with a different grouping and formation but in 6/8 jig time. It is a dance for any number of trios in a line, each gentleman having a lady on each side of him. Each set of three faces another set of three. This jig is very popular at céilíthe, especially if there are more ladies present than gentlemen as the formation requires two ladies per gentleman.

Formation
The initial line-up is shown in the sketch and the photographs.

The Harvest Time Jig Movements
Advance and retire: Each line of three takes the inside hands, the gentleman's hand underneath the lady's; using the promenade step, both lines advance towards each other (two bars), then retire

```
Gents      X

Ladies     O                           OXO  6

                                       OXO  5

                                       OXO  4

                                       OXO  3

                                       OXO  2

                                       OXO  1.

                                       TOP OF ROOM
```

Harvest Time jig starting formation.

Start of Harvest Time jig: the take-up position.

to place (two bars). The movement is then repeated (four bars, making a total of eight bars).

Sides: Dancers in each set of three hold the inside hands, then sidestep to their own right, finishing with the rising step (four bars). (Refer back to the definition of the rising step version 2 when danced at the end of a sidestep.) All sidestep back to place, finishing as before (four bars, making a total of eight bars).

Right and left hands across: Dancers in each set of six give their right hands across in the centre, the gentleman's underneath the lady's, then dance around clockwise (four bars). Then release, hands reverse, give the left hands into the centre, and dance back to the original place (four bars, making a total of eight bars).

Sides: The same as the second movement ('Sides'), except all sidestep left first. (This makes a total of eight bars.)

Left and right hands across: The same as the third movement ('Right and left hands across'), except all give their left hands into the centre first. (This makes a total of eight bars.)

Step and turn: The gentleman in the centre turns to face the lady on the right, who faces him. Both dance the 'sink and grind' step on the right foot twice (for sink and grind, see The Rising Step version 3 at the beginning of the céilí section) (four bars). The gentleman and lady each take the other's right hand, and using the promenade step both dance a full turn, then release the hands; the gentleman now faces the lady on his left (four bars). Both dance the 'sink and grind' step on the right foot twice (four bars). The gentleman takes the lady's left hand, and in promenade step, both dance a full turn into their original places (four bars). (This makes a total of sixteen bars.)

Advance, retire and pass through: Each trio takes each other's hands in a line, then advance and retire (four bars). All release hands, then advance and pass through the opposite line, passing right arm to right with the person facing, and moving on to face a new set, ready to recommence the dance (four bars, making a total of eight bars).

Finally, repeat the dance with each new set.

Cor Muirgheis: Morris Reel

The Morris Reel is an eight-hand dance for four couples in reel time. It is one of the easier eight-hand dances and is often taught to young dancers as an introduction to eight-hand dances, especially in competitions. It commences with the lead around, then the body, which has four movements; the body is followed by the first figure, which is danced firstly by top couples, followed by side couples.

The body is then performed again, followed by the second figure, first for tops, then sides. The body is again repeated, followed by the finish.

Formation

The initial line-up is shown in the sketch and the photographs.

Gents   X

Ladies   O   (2)

                                            OX

                            X   O

            (3)   O   X   (4)

                                    XO
                                    (1)

                    TOP OF ROOM.

Couple No. 1 Leading Tops   Couple No. 2 Opposite Tops
Couple No. 3 Leading sides   Couple No. 4 Opposite Sides
Couple No. 1 and 4 are Contrary to each other
Couple No. 2 and 3 are Contrary to each other.

Morris reel starting position formation.

Start of Morris reel: the take-up position.

Morris reel: opening position with the hands.

Morris reel: the hand position for the movement 'sides'.

Morris reel: close-up of hand positions for 'sides'.

Morris Reel Movements

Lead around: Each gentleman with his partner on his right-hand side takes the inside hand, the gentleman's hand underneath the lady's. Using the promenade step (which can be simple threes or skip threes – usually in competition it is skip threes), all couples dance a complete circle anticlockwise, all the way round to place, with the gentlemen on the inside. Dancers then release hands, turn inwards, and take the other inside hands (eight bars). All couples dance a complete circle clockwise back to place, again with the gentlemen on the inside. They then release hands and turn into their original place. (This is eight bars, making a total of sixteen bars.)

The Movements of the Body

Sides: Partners each take their right hand in the right, left hand in the left. Leading and opposite tops change places with the couple on the right, finishing with the sidestep with two threes (four bars). All couples then sidestep back to place (four bars). The movement is repeated, with the tops changing places with the couple on the left, and back to place. (Eight bars, making a total of sixteen bars.)

Attention: When sidestepping to the right always go behind; when sidestepping to the left go in front.

Right hands across: Using the promenade step, the ladies give their right hands across into the centre, and dance round clockwise (four bars). They then release hands, reverse turn, give their left hands into the centre, and dance back to place (four bars). Keeping their left hands in the centre, the ladies put their right hand in their partner's right hand, and all dance round anticlockwise to place. They then release their hands in the centre, and turn into place with their partner (eight bars, making a total of sixteen bars).

This movement is repeated with the gentlemen giving their right hand in the centre, and dancing the routine as above. (This makes sixteen bars, therefore thirty-two bars for the complete movement.)

Return chain: Partners face each other, each taking the other's right hand. Using the promenade step, the gentlemen go in an anticlockwise direction, the ladies clockwise. The gentlemen advance, and take the left hand of the lady on the right, then continue the chain movement, giving the right and the left hand alternately of the oncoming ladies. They continue until they meet their partner at the opposite side of the circle with the right hand, when they make a half turn (eight bars). All dancers chain back (the gentlemen clockwise) to their original place, where they meet their partner with the right hand and turn into their own place (eight bars, making a total of sixteen bars).

Back to back: Partners take each other's right hand, gentlemen sidestep on their left foot towards the left of the opposite lady, while ladies sidestep on the left foot towards the left of the opposite gentlemen (two bars); on the two threes gentlemen take the left hand of the opposite lady to form a ring of four: the gentlemen are now facing outwards, back to back, while the ladies are facing each other inwards (two bars). The gentlemen then release their partner's right hand, and make a full turn with the opposite lady (two bars). Both gentlemen then pass right shoulder to right shoulder and return to their own partner, taking their right hand in their own right hand; all turn clockwise into their original place (two bars). Partners face each other and take both hands crossed. Using the promenade step, the top

couples swing round with the couple on the left in an anticlockwise direction, revolving clockwise and so back to their original place. (Eight bars, making a total of sixteen bars.)

The four movements above form the body of the dance. This is followed by the first figure.

The First Figure

Advance and retire: Leading and opposite tops take inside hands with their partner; in the promenade step, they advance towards each other (two bars), then retire to place (two bars). The above is repeated (four bars). Both couples face each other, take their two hands crossed, swing around each other in an anticlockwise direction revolving clockwise, then back to their original place (eight bars, making a total of sixteen bars).

Now the side couples perform this figure.

Return now to the movements of the body.

This is followed by the second figure.

The Second Figure

The ladies' chain: Top ladies advance to the centre towards each other, each takes the right hand of the other in passing, then they release hands and continue to the opposite gentleman, taking his left hand in their left: both turn (four bars). They release hands, ladies return to their partner, passing right shoulder to right, take the right hand of their partner and turn into their own position (four bars). Both couples face each other, take their two hands crossed, swing around each other in an anticlockwise direction revolving clockwise, then back to their original place (eight bars, making a total of sixteen bars).

The ladies' chain is now performed by the side couples.

The body is again performed.

The Finish

All join hands in a ring, and using the promenade step, advance to the centre (two bars), then retire to place (two bars). The movement is then repeated (four bars). All sidestep anticlockwise, finishing with two threes (four bars). All then sidestep clockwise, finishing with two threes (four bars), then advance and retire as before (eight bars). All sidestep clockwise and threes (four bars), then sidestep and threes back to place (four bars). Release hands, partners face each other and take both hands crossed, then swing round to the right (eight bars, making a total of forty bars).

Lá Fhéile Phádraig: St Patrick's Day

An eight-hand dance in 6/8 jig time, danced to the tune of the same name, for four couples. The first part of the tune consists of eight bars of music, while the second part is fourteen bars, which is unusual for a céilí dance. Each part of the music is played twice after the eight-bar introduction. It has a lead around, body, two figures and a finish. Some of the movements can be found in other eight-hand céilí dances, although they may have a different number of bars depending on whether they are danced to the first part of the tune or the second part. This is a very popular dance at major competition events.

Formation

The initial line-up is shown in the sketch and the photographs.

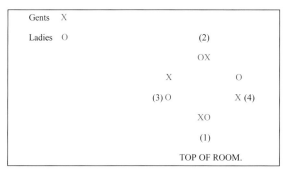

St Patrick's Day starting position formation.

Leading and opposite tops, and leading and opposite sides are numbered the same as in the Morris Reel, as are the opposite couples. The positions also remain the same. Most eight-hands have this set-up.

St Patrick's Day Movements

Lead around: The gentlemen with their partner on their right-hand side take the inside hand, his

St Patrick's Day performed by a mixed team at a world championship.

St Patrick's Day: first figure.

hand underneath hers. In the promenade step (skip threes), all couples dance a complete circle anti-clockwise until they get back to place, the gentlemen on the inside of the circle. All release hands, turn inwards, and take the other inside hand (eight bars). All now dance a complete circle clockwise (the gentlemen on the inside) until they get back to place, then release hands and turn into their original place (eight bars, making a total of sixteen bars).

Movements of the Body

Sides: Partners exchange places in sidestep, the gentlemen behind finishing with the rising step (as explained in the definition of The Rising Step, version 2), as danced at the end of a sidestep (four bars). All sidestep back to place, the gentlemen in front this time, finishing as before (four bars, making a total of eight bars).

Note: When going to the right, pass behind, when going to the left pass in front.

Half left and right: Partners face each other: each takes the other's right hand, and in promenade step, turn once in place (two bars). All release hands, the top gentleman exchanges places with the side gentleman on the left, passing left shoulder to left, and turns anticlockwise into the new position (two bars). The ladies dance in place. The top ladies now exchange places with the side lady on the left, passing right shoulder to right, and turn clockwise into the new position (two bars, making a total of six bars).

Check the diagram above for the new positions:

Top couple 1 are now in position 3
Side couple 3 are now in position 1
Top couple 2 are now in position 4
Side couple 4 are now in position 2

Sides: Repeat the first movement ('Sides') in these new places. Remember, when going to the right pass behind, and when to the left pass in front. (This makes a total of eight bars.)

Half left and right: All repeat the second movement ('Half left and right') to return to their original place, passing with the same shoulder as before; all finish facing their partner, ready for the next movement. (This makes a total of six bars.)

Double quarter chain: Partners face each other and take each other's right hand, then turn once in place (two bars). All release hands; the gentlemen then take the left hand of the lady on their left (in their original place) (two bars), then turn once in place (two bars). All return to their own partner with the right hand (two bars), and make a full turn (two bars). All release hands; the gentlemen continue to the lady on the right of their original place (two bars), then take their left hand and turn once in place (two bars). They advance to their partner with the right hand, and turn into their original place (two bars; this makes a total of sixteen bars).

Extended sides: Partners exchange places with sidestep, the gentlemen behind, finishing with the rising step (version 2) (four bars). All sidestep in the same direction, finishing as before (four bars). Each gentleman takes the right hand of the lady on the right in their own right hand, makes a full turn, then chains back to their partner with their right hand and turns into their own place (six bars; this makes a total of fourteen bars).

Full chain: Partners face each other, and take each other's right hand. In the promenade step, gentlemen dance in an anticlockwise direction, ladies clockwise. The gentlemen advance, take the left hand of the lady on the right and continue on the circle, taking the right and left hand alternately of the oncoming ladies, until all return to place. Partners take each other's right hand, and make a full turn into their original place. (This makes a total of fourteen bars.)

The First Figure: Tops

Advance and retire: This is performed as explained in the Morris Reel above. (This makes a total of sixteen bars.)

The body is again danced before the first figure for sides is danced (below) in order to fit in with the music parts.

The First Figure: Sides

Advance and retire: This is performed as explained in the Morris Reel above. (This makes a total of sixteen bars.)

The body is again danced.

The Second Figure: Tops

Ladies' chain: This is performed as explained in the Morris Reel above. (This makes a total of sixteen bars.)

The body is again performed.

The Second Figure: Sides

Ladies' chain: This is performed as explained in the Morris Reel above. (This makes a total of sixteen bars.)

The body is once more performed.

The Finish

Lead Around: Refer to the opening movement at the beginning of the dance: this is the same movement. It is then repeated. It opens and closes the dance. (This makes a total of sixteen bars.)

The explanation for the body being performed in this dance between tops and sides performing the figures is so that each movement fits the music, the first part consisting of eight bars twice, making sixteen bars, then the second part consisting of fourteen bars twice making twenty-eight bars. Each movement can be seen above the breakdown of bars, as the number of bars for each movement is given. The lead around, double quarter chain and the figures are danced to the first part of the tune, where eight bars repeated equals sixteen bars. The sides, half left and right, extended sides and the full chain are danced to the second part of the tune, making fourteen bars.

Cor Ceathrar: Four-Hand Reel

This is a four-hand dance in reel time for two couples. It consists of a lead around, a body, two figures and a lead around to finish. It is a popular céilí and competition dance.

Formation

The initial line-up is shown in the sketch and the photograph.

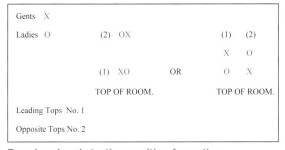

Four-hand reel starting position formation.

Movements for the Four-Hand Reel

Lead Around: Partners take their inside hands, the gentleman's hand underneath the lady's. In the promenade step, both couples dance a full circle anticlockwise all the way to place. They then release hands and turn inwards, and take the other inside hands (eight bars). Both couples now dance full circle back to place, release hands and turn into their own original place (eight bars, making a total of sixteen bars).

Four-hand reel: starting position side view.

Movements of the Body

The square: Partners exchange places in sidestep finishing with two threes, gentlemen to the right behind, ladies to the left in front; on the second two threes they turn to face their own partner (four bars). They continue in the same direction in sidestep finishing with two threes, then turn to face the opposite couple (four bars): each couple is now in the place of the opposite couple. Both couples continue the movement as above to return to their own place (eight bars, making a total of sixteen bars).

Four sevens: Each gentleman sidesteps to the right behind his partner, while the ladies sidestep to the left in front (two bars). All sidestep back to place with the gentlemen in front (two bars). The movement is then repeated (four bars, making a total of eight bars).

Note: The threes are not performed in this movement.

Right and left hands across: The four dancers give their right hands across into the centre, the gentlemen's hands underneath the ladies', and in promenade step they dance round clockwise (four bars). They then release hands, turn, and all give their left hands and dance back anticlockwise to place, finishing facing their own partner (four bars, making a total of eight bars).

Down the centre: The top couple each takes the other's right hand, then sidesteps through the centre to the place of the opposite couple, while the opposite couple sidesteps on the outside to their place (two bars). The opposite couple now

Four-hand reel: positions for the movement of the right hands across.

takes their right hands, and both couples make a half turn in place (two bars). The tops release hands, and both couples sidestep back to place, the tops going on the outside (two bars). The tops take the other's right hand again, and both couples make a half turn into their own place (two bars, making a total of eight bars).

Right and left chain: Danced to eight bars of music. In promenade step the gentlemen move in a clockwise direction and the ladies anticlockwise, the gentlemen giving their right hand to the opposite lady (two bars). They then release the right hands and continue, to meet their partner with the left hand (two bars). Now at the opposite side of the set, they continue to the opposite lady with the right hand (two bars), then to their partner with the left hand (two bars), and turn into their own place. (This makes a total of eight bars.)

The five movements above make up the body of the dance.

The First Figure

Figure of eight and the ring of three: The tops take the inside hands, and advance towards the opposite couple (two bars). They release hands, and the top gentleman dances back to place (two bars), and stands idle for the following four bars; the lady dances between the opposite couple, around the other lady,

between the couple once more, then around the gentleman; then both ladies advance to the place of the top couple (four bars). Note the opposite couple may stand idle or dance for those (eight bars).

The top couple and opposite lady form a ring and sidestep anticlockwise, finishing with two threes (four bars). They now sidestep clockwise (two bars), and on the two threes, the top couple raises their arms to form an arch, allowing the opposite lady to pass underneath to reach the place of the top lady, turning *clockwise* while the top couple advances to the opposite gentleman who has danced sidestep and threes to the right and left (two bars).

The top couple and the opposite gentleman form a ring, then sidestep clockwise, finishing with two threes (four bars). They then sidestep anticlockwise (two bars), and on the two threes raise hands to allow the opposite gentleman to pass underneath to reach the place of the top gentleman, while the top couple are turning into the new place – that is, the position of the side couple and facing each other (two bars). During that the opposite lady sidesteps to left and right.

Both couples take two hands crossed, and dance around each other in an anticlockwise direction revolving clockwise until they reach their own place (eight bars, making a total of thirty-two bars).

The opposite couple will now perform the first figure. (This makes a total of thirty-two bars.)

The body is performed again.

The Second Figure

Ladies' chain: The ladies advance towards the centre, and each takes the other's right hand. They then release, and continue to the opposite gentleman with the left hand, and both turn anticlockwise in place (four bars). They release hands, and the ladies return to their partner passing each other right shoulder to right shoulder; they take right hands with their own partner and turn into place (four bars, making eight bars in total). Both couples take two hands crossed and dance around each other in an anticlockwise direction revolving clockwise, until they reach their own place (eight bars, making a total of sixteen bars).

The body is performed again.

The Finish
The lead around: As performed at the commencement of the dance.

Geataí Dhoire: Gates of Derry

This dance originated in Co. Derry. It is an eight-hand dance in single jig time, for four couples. The formation is in two lines of four, the partners facing each other. Ordinary threes (over two threes) and *not* skip threes *must* be performed in this dance, especially in competition.

Both diagrams below are acceptable in competition.

Formation
The initial line-up is shown in the sketch and the photograph.

Gents X			
Ladies O	X O (4)		O X O X
	O X (3)		X O X O
	X O (2)	OR	(1) (2) (3) (4)
	O X (1)		
	TOP OF ROOM		TOP OF ROOM

Gates of Derry starting position formation.

In the first line, the first gentleman stands either with his left shoulder to the top of the room *or* with his back to the top of the room. In the second line the first lady stands either with her right shoulder to the top of the room, *or* facing the top of the room.

Start of Gates of Derry: the take-up position.

Movements for the Gates of Derry
Advance and retire: The dancers in line take hands, and with ordinary jump threes they advance towards each other (two bars), then retire to place (two bars). They advance again, and those in the first line raise their hands to form an arch, while those in the second line release their hands. The second line passes underneath to reach their partner's place, passing right shoulder to right shoulder, all turning clockwise into the new place (four bars). The movement is then repeated, with the second line forming the arch and the first line passing underneath to get back to their original place (eight bars). (This makes a total of sixteen bars.)

Gates of Derry: arches at the end of the advance-and-retire and the pass-through movement.

The gates: Couples no. 1 and no. 3 take crossed hands, sidestep to the gentlemen's right down the centre (two bars), and on the two threes, each gentleman releases the left hand of the lady, and turns her clockwise under his raised hand (two bars). Couples nos 1 and 3 take two hands crossed, sidestep to the gentlemen's left (two bars), and on the two threes, release hands and move into their own place (two bars). At the same time couples no. 2 and no. 4 sidestep to the gentlemen's right to the place occupied by couples no. 1 and no. 3 respectively, passing on the outside. They sidestep back to place, finishing with two short threes. (This makes a total of eight bars.)

Rings: Couples no. 1 and no. 2 take hands to form a ring, and couples no. 3 and no. 4 do likewise. They dance sidestep anticlockwise, finishing with two threes (four bars), and sidestep back to place (four bars, making a total of eight bars).

Gates of Derry: positions for the movement 'the gates': hand positions for couples no. 2 and no. 4.

1	2	3	4	starting positions
2	1	4	3	2 bars
2	4	1	3	2 bars
4	2	3	1	2 bars
4	3	2	1	2 bars = 8 bars
3	4	1	2	2 bars
3	1	4	2	2 bars
1	3	2	4	2 bars
1	2	3	4	2 bars = 16 bars

The gates: Couples no. 2 and no. 4 take crossed hands and perform the gates as described above in the second movement, then dance sidestep to the gentlemen's right, while couples no. 1 and no. 3 dance to the gentlemen's right on the outside. (This makes a total of eight bars.)

Rings: Repeat the movement as described above, but dancing sidestep clockwise first. (This makes a total of eight bars.)

Telescope: Couples no. 1 and no. 3 take uncrossed hands and dance sevens to the gentlemen's right (two bars). At the same time couples no. 2 and no. 4 dance continued sevens to the gentlemen's right on the outside, their positions now being 2 1 4 3. ('Continued sevens' is when you do *not* dance two threes at the end of a seven but continue on the same foot into next seven without a break.)

In this movement you only dance the two threes when you reach the top or end of the set. No. 1 and no. 4 (no. 4 taking uncrossed hands) change places, while no. 2 and no. 3 dance two threes in place (two bars). Their positions now are 2 4 1 3. They continue changing places as above, until all are back in their original place (twelve bars). This movement is danced with sevens, but on reaching the top and bottom of the set two threes are danced, while the two inside couples are changing places. (This makes a total of sixteen bars.)

The dancers' positions from the start and after each two bars are as follows:

Couples no. 1 and no. 4 dance 3×7s, 2×3s, 3×7s, 2×3s.

Couples no. 2 and no. 3 dance 1×7s, 2×3s, 3×7s, 2×3s, 2×7s.

Right and left hands across: Couples no. 1 and no. 2 give their right hands across in the centre, as do couples no. 3 and no. 4, and in promenade step (threes) dance forwards clockwise (four bars). They release hands, reverse and give their left hands into the centre, and dance anticlockwise to their own place. (Four bars; this makes a total of eight bars.)

Swing around: Couples no. 1 and no. 2 swing around, as do couples no. 3 and no. 4; they take both hands crossed, swing around each other in an anticlockwise direction revolving clockwise to exchange places. All couples are then in new positions, having changed lines. (This makes a total of eight bars.)

The initial line-up is shown in the photograph.

Gates of Derry: the swing around.

Advance and retire: As explained in the first movement. (This makes a total of sixteen bars.)

Note: On completion of the dance, couples no. 1 and no. 4 will have exchanged places, while couples no. 2 and no. 3 are back in their original positions.

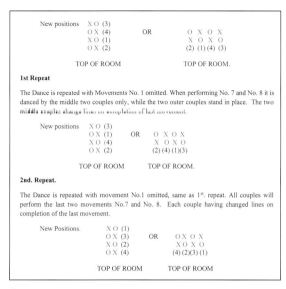

```
    New positions   X O  (3)
                    O X  (4)      OR           O  X  O  X
                    X O  (1)                   X  O  X  O
                    O X  (2)                 (2) (1) (4) (3)

              TOP OF ROOM              TOP OF ROOM.
```

1st Repeat

The Dance is repeated with Movements No. 1 omitted. When performing No. 7 and No. 8 it is danced by the middle two couples only, while the two outer couples stand in place. The two middle couples change lines on completion of last movement.

```
    New positions   X O  (3)
                    O X  (1)      OR        O  X  O  X
                    X O  (4)                X  O  X  O
                    O X  (2)              (2) (4) (1)(3)

              TOP OF ROOM         TOP OF ROOM.
```

2nd. Repeat.

The Dance is repeated with movement No.1 omitted, same as 1st. repeat. All couples will perform the last two movements No.7 and No. 8. Each couple having changed lines on completion of the last movement.

```
    New Positions.   X O  (1)
                     O X  (3)     OR         O X O X
                     X O  (2)                X O X O
                     O X  (4)              (4) (2)(3) (1)

              TOP OF ROOM         TOP OF ROOM
```

Gates of Derry: the swing around showing the new, the first repeat and the second repeat positions.

Turas 'un Tí: Trip to the Cottage

This is one of the most popular céilí dances in céilí competitions. It is not often danced at céilíthe as it is quite complex. It is an eight-hand dance in 6/8 jig time for four couples, and is danced to the tune of the same name. The dance originated in Co. Armagh.

Formation

The initial line-up is shown in the sketch.

```
    Gents   X

    Ladies  O                               (2)

                                         O  X

                               X                   O

                         (3) O                   X (4)

                                       X  O

                                        (1)

                              TOP  of  ROOM

    Couples  no.1 and no.2   Leading and Opposite Tops

    Couples  no.3 and no.4   Leading and Opposite Sides.
```

Trip to the Cottage starting position formation.

Movements for Trip to the Cottage

Cross-over and lead around: Gentlemen start with the ladies on their right-hand side. All couples take their inside hands, and in the promenade step, and all continuously dancing, the top couples change places, the gentlemen passing left shoulder to left shoulder (two bars). Side couples change places in a similar manner (two bars). Top couples then dance back to place (two bars), and all dance two threes in place (two bars). All couples lead round in an anti-clockwise direction, with side couples in place (four bars). Top couples return to place (two bars). All dance in place (two bars), couples finishing in their original places. (This makes a total of sixteen bars.)

Repeat the above movement with the *side* couples changing places first. (This makes a total of sixteen bars.)

Movements for the Body

Diagonal lines and rings: Top gentlemen take their partner's inside hand and the right hand of the lady on the left. While the two side gentlemen

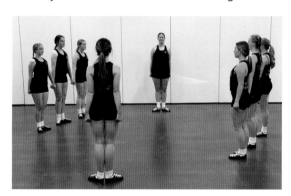

Trip to the Cottage: positions for the diagonal lines.

Trip to the Cottage: positions for the rings.

are standing in place, the trios dance towards each other, diagonally across the set in the promenade step (two bars), and retire (two bars). This movement is repeated (four bars). Each trio then takes hands to form a ring, they sidestep clockwise while the side gentleman sidesteps to the right (two bars); all dance two threes, allowing the side gentlemen to come into the ring between the two ladies (two bars). All sidestep anticlockwise, and on the two threes they release hands, face their partner and take their two hands uncrossed.

All are now in a diagonal line across the set (four bars). Couples no. 1 and no. 3 swing round each other in an anticlockwise direction, revolving clock-

Trip to the Cottage: the couples position for the swing round.

Trip to the Cottage: couples return to their original place at the end of the swing round.

wise back to their original position. At the same time couples no. 2 and no. 4 do likewise (eight bars; this makes a total of twenty-four bars).

Note: Forward and backward movement is *not* allowed while swinging in the above last eight bars. When swinging, it is acceptable for partners to dance on the same foot or on the opposite foot to their partner. Side couples perform the above movement with the top lady on the left. (This makes a total of twenty-four bars.)

The First Figure

Arches and rings: The lady of the second tops advances, and takes the left hand of the gentleman of the first tops in her right hand; the first tops raise their arms to form an arch, allowing the lady to pass underneath, and the top gentleman under his own. The lady of the first tops now passes under the arch, and the gentleman passes under again, and the lady of the second tops passes under the arch as before (eight bars). The three now take the gentleman of the second tops into the ring between the two ladies. The four sidestep anticlockwise to finish with two threes (four bars).

The following movement is performed to four bars of music, without releasing the hands. The second tops passes under the arch of the first tops and passes outwards under their own arch. The first tops pass out under their own arch, and backwards under the arch of the second tops, all facing into the ring (four bars). All sidestep clockwise, finishing with two threes (four bars). They release hands, then both couples take their two hands crossed and swing back to their own place (four bars, making a total of twenty-four bars.)

The movement is repeated, the lady of the first tops advancing to the second tops (this takes twenty-four bars).

The movement is repeated, the lady of the second sides advancing to the first sides (this takes twenty-four bars).

The movement is repeated, the lady of the first sides advancing to the second sides (this takes twenty-four bars).

The body is performed again.

The Second Figure

Advance, retire and cross over: Leading and opposite tops take their inside hands, and in the promenade step advance towards each other (two bars), then retire to place (two bars). They repeat the movement (four bars). Ladies advance towards the couple on the left, between and round the gentleman, then advance to the opposite side couple passing right shoulder to right shoulder, between and round the gentleman and back to their own place (eight bars). At the same time the gentlemen advance towards the side couple on the right (a fraction behind the lady), between and round the lady, then advance to the opposite side couple, passing left shoulder to left, between and round the lady and back to their own place. The side couples stand idle while the top couples perform the figure. (This makes a total of sixteen bars.)

The side couples now perform the second figure. The top couples stand idle while the side couples perform the figure. (This makes a total of sixteen bars.)

The body is performed again.

The Finish

Repeat the opening movement (a total of thirty-two bars).

Bainis Uí Lonagáin: Lannigan's Ball

This is a round dance in single jig time for six couples, danced to the tune of the same name. Both ordinary simple two threes, and skip two threes are acceptable. The sidestep is not performed in this dance.

Note: In competition it is acceptable to dance this as an eight-hand dance.

Formation

The initial line-up is shown in the sketch.

Movements for Lannigan's Ball

Ring: In a circle holding hands, in the promenade step, all dance round clockwise (eight bars). All then return anticlockwise, release hands, and back to place (eight bars, making a total of sixteen bars).

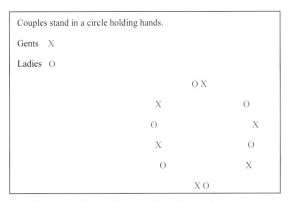

Lannigan's Ball starting position formation.

Quarter's hook: Gentlemen link their right arm in the right arm of the lady on the left, and turn once clockwise (two bars). They release arms, and link their left arm with their partner, and turn anticlockwise (two bars). They repeat the link with the lady on the left and their partner, and finish facing the lady on the left (four bars, making a total of eight bars).

Rise and grind: The gentlemen are facing the lady on the left to commence this movement. All dance the rise and grind step on the right and left foot (four bars); (for this step *see* the beginning of Chapter 5, Céilí Dancing under the section The Rising Step). Continue with throw out, hop back right foot, throw out, hop back left foot (two bars); finish with the rise and grind step on the right foot. On the 1, 2, 3, 4 movement all turn to face their partner (two bars). Dancers repeat the movement facing their partner, except they start the rise and grind step on the left foot first, and finish facing the centre (eight bars, making a total of sixteen bars).

Lead round in centre: Using the promenade step, the ladies dance round clockwise in a small circle, without taking hands (three bars), then turn right (one bar). They dance back towards their own place, taking their partner's right hand, and turn him ready to dance the movement (four bars). The gentlemen now promenade anticlockwise (three bars), then turn left (one bar). They dance back to place clockwise, take the right hand of their partner and turn into their original position. Partners face each other ready for the next movement (four bars, making a total of sixteen bars).

Flirtation: Partners take both hands *uncrossed*, and swing clockwise once in place (two bars). With the ladies remaining in their own place, the gentlemen move to the ladies on the right of their original position, take their hands uncrossed, and swing once in place. This movement continues with each lady in the ring until they reach their own place. The gentlemen form a circle facing their partner with their backs to the centre (fourteen bars, making a total of sixteen bars).

Stack-up: While the gentlemen clap hands in rhythm (two claps to each bar), the ladies dance round clockwise on the outside in the promenade step until they reach their place (six bars). Partners take both hands uncrossed and turn the gentleman into his place, the ladies now with their backs to the centre (two bars). This movement is repeated with the gentlemen dancing clockwise on the outside, while the ladies clap hands twice to each bar (six bars). Partners then take both hands uncrossed, turn and finish in the lead-around position, with the gentleman on the inside of the circle, ready for the next movement (two bars). (This makes a total of sixteen bars.)

Lead around: In the promenade step, all dance round anticlockwise, the gentlemen on the inside until they reach their own place, finishing in a circle holding hands ready for the next movement. (This makes a total of eight bars.)

Ring: Repeat the first movement ('Ring') to complete the dance. (This makes a total of sixteen bars.)

Lannigan's Ball: positions for the stack-up.

Na Trí Fionn: The Three Tunes

This is an eight-hand dance for four couples; it originated in Co Armagh. It is danced to three different tunes: 'Haste to the Wedding' (jig), 'Leslie's Hornpipe' and 'The German Beau' (reel). The reel is taken more slowly than the jig, and the hornpipe slightly more slowly still.

Formation
As in the Morris Reel, the initial line-up is shown in the sketch.

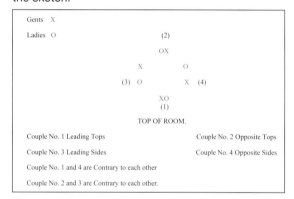

The Three Tunes starting position formation.

Then all hold hands in a ring.

The Three Tunes: rings, the opening movement.

Movements for The Three Tunes
Ring, danced to the tune 'Haste to the Wedding': All dancers take hands to form a ring, then sidestep clockwise, finishing with two threes (four bars). All sidestep back to place (four bars). Then sidestep

anticlockwise, finishing with two threes (four bars), and sidestep back to place; on the two threes all release hands and finish in their own place (four bars). (Total sixteen bars.)

Ladies' and gentlemen's ring: The ladies advance to the centre to form a ring, and then in promenade step, dance around clockwise; they release hands and finish in place. The gentlemen stand idle (four bars). All clap hands twice (one bar). Partners change places, the gentlemen behind (count one, two, three – one bar), then sidestep back to place, the gentlemen in front (two bars). Repeat the above movement with the gentlemen advancing to the centre to form the ring, while the ladies stand idle for the first four bars (eight bars). (This makes a total of sixteen bars.)

Lead around, danced to the tune 'Leslie's Hornpipe': As explained in the Morris Reel. (Total sixteen bars.)

Stamp and clap: All dancers stamp the right foot, left foot, and right again (one bar) counting one two three, then clap the hands three times (one bar). Partners change places with sidestep, the gentlemen behind (two bars). All sidestep back to place, the gentlemen in front (two bars), then clap hands alternately five times on the legs above the knee, starting with the right hand (one bar), counting one two three four five; then clap their own hands three times (one bar). The above movement is repeated (eight bars). (This makes a total of sixteen bars.)

See-saw, danced to the tune 'German Beau': Partners face each other, take both hands uncrossed, and in promenade step, swing round the set in an anticlockwise direction, revolving clockwise (eight bars). All swing round clockwise, revolving anticlockwise in a similar manner, to their original position (eight bars). (This makes a total of sixteen bars.)

Note: Movement of the arms up and down is *not* allowed in the above movement. Promenade step on the same foot or the opposite foot to the partner is acceptable.

Roly poly: All dancers close hands and raise them to chest level with the elbows bent (the right arm in front). Roll them round each other in a forward direction (one bar), then roll them back in the opposite direction (one bar). When performing roly poly, roll the forearm round each other, not just the fists, and count 'one two three four five' to each bar ('one two three four five' forward roll equals one bar, and back 'one two three four five' equals one bar).

Pivot once to the right on the right heel (one bar), and clap hands once (one bar). Gentlemen raise the right fist forwards in the air in a threatening manner, and bring it back to their side. At the same time they stamp the right foot and move forwards (one bar). They do likewise with the left hand and the left foot, moving forwards (one bar), and stamp right, left, right, turning right towards their partner (one bar). They clap hands three times towards their partner, while the ladies turn their head away to the right (one bar). Partners change places with sidestep, the gentlemen behind (two bars), and sidestep back to

The Three Tunes: the roly poly.

The Three Tunes: close-up of arm positions for the roly poly.

place, the gentlemen in front (two bars). (This makes a total of twelve bars.)

Note: In the last four bars there are no 'two threes' between the sevens.

The above movement is repeated. (This makes a total of twelve bars.)

Hook and chain, danced to the tune 'Haste to the Wedding': Each gentleman faces the lady on the left, both hook their left arm in the other's left arm, and in promenade step, turn once in place, with the gentlemen going in an anticlockwise direction. They take the right hand of their partner in their own right hand, then release and advance taking the left hand of the lady on the right. They continue the chain movement, giving their right hand, then their left hand alternately to the hands of the oncoming ladies, until they reach their own place. Finally the gentlemen take the right hand of their partner and turn into their original position. (This makes a total of sixteen bars.)

Ladies and gentlemen's ring: As explained in the second movement 'Ladies and gentlemen's ring'. (This makes a total of sixteen bars.)

Sides under arms, danced to the tune 'Leslie's Hornpipe': Partners take their inside hands and in promenade step, the top couples raise their hands to form an arch and change places with the couple on the left, allowing them to pass under the arch (two bars). All release hands, turn in, and take the other inside hands (two bars). All couples return to place, then the side couples raise the hands, and the top couples pass under the arch. All release hands and turn into their own place (four bars). The movement is repeated with the top couples now changing with the couple on the right, and raising their hands to form the arch first (eight bars). (This makes a total of sixteen bars.)

Stamp and clap: As explained in the fourth movement, 'Stamp and clap'. (This makes a total of sixteen bars.)

Thread the needle, danced to the tune 'German Beau': All take hands to form a ring except the gentleman of the first tops and the lady of the first sides. The lady of the first sides advances, and passes under the arch of the first tops with all other dancers following round the set in an anticlockwise direction until they reach their own place, and the lady of the first tops passes under her own arch (eight bars). The movement is repeated with the gentleman of the first tops passing under the arch of the first sides, all following clockwise until they reach their own place and the gentleman of the first sides passes under his own arch (eight bars). (This makes a total of sixteen bars.)

Roly poly: As explained in the sixth movement, 'Roly poly'. (Total twenty-four bars.)

Ring, danced to the tune 'Haste to the Wedding': As explained in the first movement, 'Ring, danced to the tune "Haste to the Wedding"'. (Total sixteen bars.)

An Rince Mór

This is a round dance in reel time for any number of couples. It is known only by the Gaelic title 'Rince Mór', which means 'Big Dance'. This dance was popularly used as the 'last dance' at céilithe, especially in the North of Ireland.

Formation

Couples hold hands in a circle. The initial line-up is shown in the sketch.

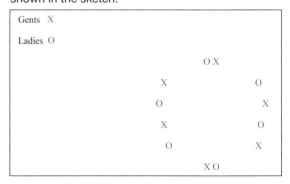

An Rince Mór starting position formation.

Movements for Rince Mór

Ring to left and right: All dancers, holding hands, sidestep clockwise and finish with two threes (four bars). All sidestep anticlockwise finishing as before, and release hands in place (four bars, making a total of eight bars).

Swing with the lady on the left: Gentlemen take crossed hands with the lady on the left, and swing clockwise in place. (Total eight bars.)

Swing with partner: Gentlemen take crossed hands with their partner, and swing clockwise in place. (Total eight bars.)

Link arms: Gentlemen link their right arm in the right arm of the lady on the left, and turn once (two bars). They release arms, then link the left arm with their partner, and turn once (two bars). They then link their right arm with the lady on the left, and turn once (two bars). Partners take both hands crossed, the ladies make a half turn, so the gentlemen are now on the inside in preparation for the next movement (two bars, making a total of eight bars).

Lead around: With the couples now in lead-around position, all dancers promenade anticlockwise (six bars). During the last two bars all form a ring ready to recommence the dance. (This makes a total of eight bars.)

This concludes the section on the céilí dances most popular at céilíthe and most frequently performed in competitive Irish dancing. This section provides an excellent variety and insight into the range of the movements and steps performed in céilí dancing.

St Patrick's Day: the highlight of the team's career.

CHAPTER 6

EXAMINATIONS, QUALIFICATIONS AND COMPETITIONS

I feel that the essence of dance is the expression of man – the landscape of his soul. I hope that every dance I do reveals something of myself or some wonderful thing a human can be.

Martha Graham

Irish dancing, like most sport/teaching activities, is a highly competitive hobby, tightly controlled by the various regulatory bodies. Each has their own well established and strict procedures in place. Whilst most of the Irish dancing organizations, identified earlier, have similar qualifications and examinations, there are some differences in some of the detail – although essentially, they all use similar models. The following section is based on the systems in place for CLRG, and are summarized below; the full details can be found on their website.[8] There can also be slight variations in the procedures and practices between different countries and regions within the CLRG family, and it is therefore advisable to check the precise detail for individual areas as they are frequently revised and updated.

EXAMINATIONS

Regulations

An Coimisiún le Rincí Gaelacha has a long established examination authority – An t-Údarás Scrúdaithe – to administer examination affairs on behalf of the organization. When an examination

is being arranged, An t-Údarás Scrúdaithe selects an examination panel from the approved pool of SDCRG examiners. The normal number making up the full panel or Board of Examiners is approximately thirty-six from all over the world; however, this may vary from time to time due to retirements and delays in appointing replacements. Any member of the Board of Examiners may be chosen to act as an examiner for TMRF (céilí teaching), TCRG (teacher), ADCRG (adjudicator), BG (grade examiner) or SDCRG (examiner) qualifications. Grade examiners are permitted to examine graded exams for dancers up to and including Grade 10, as long as there have been at least four different grade examiners involved in the process. Only SDCRG examiners may officiate at Grades 11 and 12, with a different SDCRG examining each level.

An t-Údarás Scrúdaithe arranges and organizes all aspects of An Coimisiún examinations, and is responsible for the following:

- Setting examination dates.
- Selection of examination venues.
- Arrangement of timetables.
- Selection of examination panels from the Board of Examiners.
- Specifying closing dates for applications.
- Confirmation and notification of examination results.
- Conditions of entry.
- Examination syllabi.

- Systems of examination.
- Qualifying marks.

It is also responsible for certifying all examination results, and provides a regular report to An Coimisiún on the work of the committee recently completed and its future plans. It also provides the statistics of the number of candidates and the percentage of successes and failures. In addition, the authority is responsible for the provision of comprehensive training of new examiners. When an examination panel has completed their examination of candidates and results have been compiled and collated, the results are submitted to the examination authority for sanctioning and the certification of results. It is the norm that the overall percentages of successful candidates are notified to the main body of CLRG before being communicated to the individual candidates.

Qualifications

A number of different levels of examination are readily available under the auspices of CLRG. The first set of examinations is aimed at defining the examinees' level of competence through a grading system. Most dance schools participate in the grade examination process as this provides a method of measuring progress outside competition. These start at the beginner level and then become more demanding as the candidates' skill, knowledge and ability increases. They graduate through a number of levels to Grade 12, the highest level available for the enthusiastic amateur. Success at the highest level in the grading system is also a requirement before sitting the formal teaching examinations.

Formal qualifications are necessary

- For teachers to enter pupils in a registered feis.
- For adjudicators to judge at officially sanctioned competitions.
- For examiners to participate in exams for teachers and adjudicators.

These qualifications are awarded following successful written and practical examinations. The following formal qualifications are currently available:

TMRF: The first level of a teaching qualification, necessary for the holder to teach céilí dancing in a registered school and to enter competitions.

TCRG: The second level of teaching, which allows the holder to teach all dance forms in a registered school and to enter officially registered competitions. Candidates can elect to bypass the TMRF qualification as the TCRG qualifications examine both solo step dancing and céilí dancing knowledge and expertise.

ADCRG: The third level of qualification, which is necessary for the holder to participate as an adjudicator at an officially registered competition.

BG: The fourth level of qualification, allowing a qualified adjudicator to examine at grade exams up to Level 10.

SDCRG: The fifth level and the highest qualification – this allows the holder to officiate at all the exams outlined above, as well as participate at exams for new SDCRGs.

Grade Examinations

General

This section is a summary of the system operated by CLRG. Full details can be found on the CLRG website.[8]

The purpose of the Grade Examinations Scheme is to provide a structured framework within which dancers can progress towards an achievable goal. The syllabus is designed to provide a strong foundation in Irish dance by developing a candidate's physical skills, expression and musicality, and an appreciation and knowledge of the traditional dances and culture. It provides a worthwhile sense of achievement for individuals, whether they dance solely for health, recreation or competitive reasons, or hope to pursue a career in Irish dancing.

Grade examinations are unlike competitions in that each candidate is individually examined and receives a detailed written assessment of their performance and knowledge of the grade being attempted. These examinations are open to both male and female candidates regardless of age and ability. Those wishing to sit further CLRG examinations must have successfully completed Grades 1 to 12.

The scheme consists of an optional preliminary grade followed by a further twelve grades, with each grade becoming increasingly more demanding on the candidate's skill, knowledge and ability. Each grade must be passed, and a certificate awarded before a candidate may attempt the next level. The specific requirements for each grade, and the rules governing the conduct of the examinations, can be found on the website.

Teaching Examinations

Again, this section is a summary of the system operated by CLRG. Full details can be found on the CLRG website,[8] and cover the two teacher qualifications available.

TCRG Examinations

The most frequently sat examination is for the TCRG qualification, so the requirements are detailed below, and then the differences for the TMRF are highlighted.

- The entry requirements include age, and proof of having succeeded in the grade exams.
- The candidate's competency and suitability must be demonstrated, including a recommendation from a qualified teacher, and confirmation that the candidate can perform the necessary dances to an acceptable standard.
- Dates and locations for exams.
- Examination content, which for a TCRG consists of the following:
  - A written céilí test: candidates are expected to have a detailed knowledge of all the dances in 'Ár Rincí Céilí'.
  - A written music test: candidates are asked to answer questions about the name, the timing and the number of bars of nineteen set dance tunes.
  - A practical test in solo dancing: candidates are expected to dance a number of selected dances – refer to the syllabus for details.
  - A practical test in teaching solo dancing: candidates are expected to teach steps from selected light and heavy dances – refer to the syllabus for details.
  - A practical test in teaching céilí dancing: candidates must be prepared to teach selected dances from 'Ár Rincí Céilí'.
  - An Irish language test if applicable: this is compulsory for candidates residing in Ireland, and involves demonstrating a knowledge of, conversing in, and reading the Irish language with an emphasis on themselves and dancing terms and matters.
- Communication of results: these will be e-mailed to candidates after certification with marks in each section.
- Terms for repeat examination.

A detailed knowledge of CLRG's child protection policy and vetting procedures is also required – more details of these are covered in Chapter 9.

TMRF Examinations

The details for the TMRF examinations are very similar, albeit somewhat simpler, to those for the TCRG; the major difference is that the examination content consists of only three sections:

- The written céilí dancing test – as for TCRG.
- The practical test in teaching céilí dancing – as for TCRG.
- The oral Irish language test, if applicable – as for TCRG.

All required sections must be attempted at the same examination (subject to the exception relating to the Irish language test in the case of persons living outside Ireland).

Adjudication Examination

The ADCRG Exam

This section is a summary of the system operated by CLRG. The ADCRG is the most demanding of the CLRG exams: full details can be found on the CLRG website[8] but the major additional factors are described below.

Qualifications for entry: The examination is open to persons who are thirty years of age or older at the date of their application. They must already have passed the TCRG examination; they must be currently registered with An Coimisiún Le Rincí Gaelacha; and they must have been an active teacher while officially registered with CLRG for a period of five full years. The teaching experience must have occurred within the three years prior to submitting the application.

Examination content: This consists of five sections:

- A written ceili dancing test – as for TCRG.
- A written music test – as for TCRG.
- A practical test in the adjudicating of step dancing and céilí dancing, including an interview.
- A written maths test on adding and transcribing marks, determining the position from marks, and operating the official points system for judging.
- An oral Irish language test if applicable – as for TCRG.

Repeat exams: There are strict requirements for repeat examinations following a failure at the first attempt. These depend on the magnitude of the failure and the timings of the proposed resit.

Conduct: There are also strict regulations enforced for the conduct of the examination. Prospective candidates are strongly advised to study these, as contravention might result in disqualification.

Triall Moltóireachta: Adjudication Test
The Mini Feis
In this test candidates are required to demonstrate their ability to judge competitions in both step dancing and céilí dancing. A special mini feis is held in which dancers actually compete for prizes, as happens at an ordinary feis. The competitions are judged, and prizes awarded by a qualified adjudicator. The mini-feis programme consists of eight competitions in various age groups and grades.

The examination candidates judge the competitions, and take notes of competitors' strong points and also their weak points, faults and so on. They award marks and place the competitors in order of merit. It should be clear from the notes why one competitor is placed higher or lower than another.

The Interview
Following the mini feis, each candidate is interviewed by the panel of examiners. About thirty minutes before the interview the mark sheets are returned to allow the candidate to refresh his or her memory on the competitions, comments and so on. At the interview the candidate answers questions from the examiners on his or her results, marks and comments, and if requested, gives the reasons for particular placings. Basically, the candidate is required to justify his or her results to the panel. Candidates are advised to attend as many feiseanna as possible to gain experience of adjudicating before taking the exam.

Exam Marking
Detailed advice on the criteria used in assessing marks is outlined in the CLRG website, and candidates are again advised to familiarize themselves with these. The Triall i Suimiú marcanna agus fail torthaí is a maths test that tests the candidates' ability to add marks, place competitors in order on the basis of marks, and to use the official points system to determine overall results. Candidates may use calculators in these tests, and may refer to a schedule of points provided by the examiners in charge.

PREPARING FOR EXAMS

In general, Irish dancing exams are different from other exams in that they have a much higher proportion of practical tests. However, there are some general areas that are relevant whatever the exam, and it is well worthwhile paying attention to and revising for these as well as those specific to the Irish dancing exam.

General Tips
Prepare your Study Programme
Initially, identify the topics that you are going to revise and prepare a programme of work, with a timetable and milestones, so you can self-monitor your progress. Ensure that you allow yourself enough time to achieve your schedule: don't leave it all until the last minute. While some examinees seem to thrive on last-minute cramming, it is widely

accepted that for the majority of applicants this is not the best way to prepare for an exam.

Identify and Organize your Revision Areas

Identify where you are going to do your bookwork and your practical dancing rehearsals. Regarding bookwork, factors such as space, light and comfortable furniture are important. Also ensure you have sufficient stationery and computer aids available. Clear your study room of potential distractions so you can fully focus on the task in hand. It is most likely that your dancing exam will involve some practical work for both dancing yourself and for teaching others – decide where you are going to do this, and select who is going to help. Your dancing friends and qualified teachers are a better option than parents for this role. You will need expert feedback. Check on the availability of your dance school or dance studio, and reserve your practice time well in advance.

Start your Revision Early

There is no substitute for starting revision early. Prepare your plan as soon as you have registered for your exam. You need to give yourself enough time to review everything that you have been taught, and make sure that you understand it – if not, check it out with your teacher. As said earlier, cramming in the final week is not very productive. It is recommended that you review each subject as you go, as this will make revision much easier. Ultimately, success comes from studying hard and knowing your subject, and starting early is the best way to achieve this.

Look after yourself throughout Revision, Rehearsal and Exam Time

You will be able to work better if you eat a healthy diet and get plenty of exercise and sleep. This is particularly true when preparing for exams, as there will be extra pressure and stress on you. This applies not only whilst you are preparing for the exam, but also over the exam period itself. Living on junk food, whilst this may be convenient, is not a good idea, and it is far better to follow the diet advice given in Chapter 9.[24] It is also a good idea to take regular exercise when doing your bookwork – a brisk walk will get your blood moving and ensure that you are better able to concentrate. (Again, there is more about this in Chapter 9.) When doing practical rehearsal work always do your warm-up exercises before starting dancing practice (again, more information and advice is given in Chapter 9).

Vary your Revision Techniques

Variety is the spice of life, and it helps to improve your studying. Always doing the same thing, such as reading over the same notes on a subject, is likely to become quite dull and boring. Change your revision routine by trying different exercises and techniques – take periodic opportunities to practise papers and questions to test yourself and your knowledge. Your dance teachers will be very happy to mark these for you, as they, too, will be wanting you to be successful. If you know of other dancers who are taking the exam, arrange to participate in discussion groups – after all, they are not competing with you, you are all competing with the exam.

Take Regular Breaks

Continuous work for eight hours can be unproductive – it is very hard to work in a concentrated way for more than a few hours. Some days you will be able to do more than others, but usually regular two- to three-hour sessions are likely to be the most beneficial; also, take ten- to fifteen-minute breaks now and again to have a drink or walk around.

Know your Exam

First, make sure that you know the syllabus for your exam – the topics that are included, and the full range of possible activities required in the practical sections. Obtain some past papers, look at these and practise them. Check for the exam type, whether it is multiple choice, short answer or essay. In most Irish dancing exams short answers are required, but be sure to check beforehand. Ensure that you know what you might be expected to do – for example, how many questions from each section you will have to answer, and how much time you will have to complete them.

Obviously, on the day it is crucial that you read and follow the instructions on the paper itself, or listen carefully to those issued by the examiner at the time. Never rush to start answering the questions – take five minutes to read them fully, noting how many marks are given for each question. Quickly assess your ability to score highly, and plan your answering strategy to maximize your marks and ultimate success.

Familiarize yourself with the Logistical Details for your Exam

It may seem obvious, but do make sure that you are fully familiar with all the practicalities relating to the exam day. Some of the following are key:

- The location and venue, and how you are going to get there – it is not unknown for candidates to go to the wrong venue!
- The timetable – the starting time and exam duration. Do you need to get there early, for example, in order to register?
- What time do you need to leave to be there on time? Always allow a contingency period, as it is far better to arrive early, rather than risk missing the exam by being late.
- What do you need to take with you? This might include pencils, pens, calculators, ID.
- What do you do if something goes wrong on the day? For example, you might be taken ill or get held up in traffic congestion – you need to know who to contact in this eventuality.

In addition to the general tips above, an Irish dancing exam will require you to concentrate on other unique but specific areas. The TCRG exam includes both practical solo dancing and the teaching of a class of dancers as well as written tests, so you will need to be both physically and mentally fit. I recommend adoption of a 'SAP' programme as preparation to cover both the written and practical elements of the exam. To formulate this you will need to study the principles and recommendations as outlined in Chapter 9 to enable you to fully appreciate and understand what is meant by a 'SAP' programme.

A 'SAP' Programme for a TCRG Exam

'SAP' stands for Strength, Agility and Preparation. The summary below can be used to prepare for a specific project or assignment, such as taking the TCRG examination. It might be called a roadmap to a successful exam result.

Strength

You will need to develop and improve your strength in three key areas: mind, body and emotion.[25]

Mind: Set your focus to conquer any fears and weaknesses you may have regarding your knowledge and concerns about sitting examinations.

Body: Prepare your body with correct nutrition and a balanced diet – to perform at your best you need to be well fuelled for rehearsals and exam performances.

Emotion: Control your emotion by changing stress to vitality, to allow you to go the full distance from exam application to exam execution.

Agility

You will need to concentrate on the three areas of physicality, stamina and dance.

Physicality: You need to be fully fit to enable improvement in your agility fitness and all round performance and to avoid injury.

Stamina: Build up your stamina progressively over a period before the exam to reach peak fitness. This will help you to achieve your full potential for the dancing and teaching questions in the exam.

Dance: Regularly practise all the steps and dances you might be asked to dance and/or teach to ensure you are able to perform and teach the movements and routines correctly.

Preparation

All teachers and examiners will advise that being fully prepared is essential to ultimate success in examinations. Full awareness, understanding and familiarization of the scope, detail and syllabus of the relevant exam modules for the TCRG (or other) exam is crucial. You will specifically need to study for the tests described below.

The written music test: You will need to identify a large number of set dance tunes from their music, together with the timing and the number of bars in the step and the set and other features. Therefore you will need to be familiar with all set dance tunes.

The written céilí dancing paper: You will need to have a detailed knowledge of all the thirty dances in the official TCRG handbook.

Practical solo teaching: You will be required to teach and perhaps dance a light and heavy step to a group of dancers. Also, you will need to demonstrate how you would teach beginners, correct faults and teach basic movements.

Practical céilí teaching: You will be required to teach and perhaps dance parts of different dances to a group of dancers. You will therefore need to get as much practical experience as possible of teaching the dances beforehand.

Dancing: You will be required to perform a number of different dances, so check which dances you need to prepare for.

Irish language test: If you live in Ireland, or plan to teach there, at some stage you will need to take the Irish language test.

You will also need to prepare for the maths test and for the mini feis.

Above all, be prepared!

COMPETITIONS

Irish dancing competitions are a vitally important part of the Irish dancing scene. Whilst there are social and non-competitive aspects in some local fun events, the main drive and focus in most Irish dancing schools is competition. Initially this is usually based within the school itself, in the form of class competitions. This is where the novice/beginner starts their competition journey. This then extends to the local areas, then spreads through the regions, on to national, international and ultimately world event championships. As well as competitions for different levels there are also competitions for both males and females and for different age groups.

Competitions locally and regionally cover all abilities from novices to champions. The national, international and world events cater for championship level dancers and include competitions in solo dancing, céilí dancing, figure choreography and dance drama. To achieve a world championships qualification it is necessary to participate in solo dancing at either regional or one of the designated qualifying events. For the other categories, as in the team events, dancers only need perform at regional qualifying events.

The Main Competition Events
Typical Feiseanna
The main competition levels at day-to-day feiseanna are as follows (note that some regions vary slightly):

- Novice (beginner).
- Primary.
- Intermediate.
- Preliminary Championship.
- Open Championship.

The rules, regulations and conditions for each of these groups can be obtained from the individual region, organization or dance school – again, they may vary slightly. Each local event is registered with its own regional council, which in turn registers it with CLRG or their own head organization. The competitions not only cater for the above categories, but also for males and females. Ages range from five years of age up to senior level, which is usually over twenty or twenty-one. In some countries, particularly those in Europe and in North America, there is still a great demand for competitions in older age groups. These are for mature adults who have either taken up dancing later in life, or have returned to classes after having a family, or as a hobby or a social event, or as a means to keep fit.

Championship Events
The next level of events consists mainly of solo dancing championships, céilí and choreography, and some include dance drama. These are all at

The full range of emotions experienced during a major championship.

championship level competitions. Regional quali-fiers for the world championships take place in individual regions and countries and are officially known as regional Oireachtaisí.

Next come national championships: for example, Ireland annually hosts the oldest event in the world – The All Ireland Championships (Oireachtas Rince na hÉireann), which is open to a world-wide entry and is a very prestigious event. The Irish Nationals are also held annually, although entries are confined to residents of Ireland.

The main events in the UK are the British National-als, which are open to all, the Great Britain's (open to all) and the All Scotland's (open to all). Other national events are held in Australia, Europe, North America and New Zealand. These are run under their own regulations but under the auspices of CLRG.

Finally, the highest level of competition is the world championship.

Adjudication

All officially registered Irish dance competitions/feiseanna can only be judged by qualified adju-dicators. The number of adjudicators employed depends on the size of the event.

Grade competitions are usually judged by one adjudicator, whereas a championship competition must employ at least three adjudicators, and this can increase to five or even seven at the most prestigious events. Some events use a rotating panel system, where the adjudicators for the panel are changed for each round. So competitors can end up being judged with any number from nine to fifteen, or possibly twenty-one, depending on whether the organizers use three, five or seven adjudicators per round (there are three rounds to a championship event). Cham-pionships and titles at these high levels are very competitive, and every attempt is made to ensure that the judging process is as fair and as accurate as possible. The World Championships have the largest number of dancer entries, and have been known to use as many as over forty adjudicators in the event.

Very tight rules govern judging at all competi-tions under the jurisdiction of CLRG; full details of all these rules can be found in the CLRG website.[8] Only an adjudicator currently registered with An Coimisiún may adjudicate at their registered events. Furthermore there are a number of additional rules under which an adjudicator may not be allowed to judge – for example the association rule, where an adjudicator has a professional relationship with a competing school.

An adjudicator must also have been registered as an adjudicator for two years immediately prior

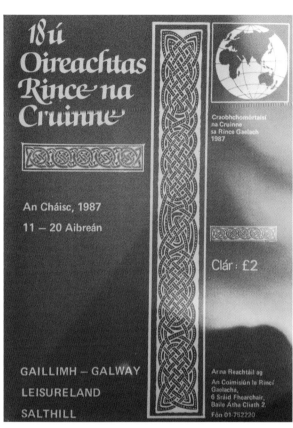

The programme for the 18th World Championship held in Galway 1987.

The programme for the 48th World Championship held in Glasgow 2018.

to the Oireachtas Rince na hÉireann (All Ireland Championship) or the Oireachtas Rince na Cruinne (World Championships) in order to be eligible to apply to adjudicate at these events. An adjudicator must also have judged at least one registered feis, which has included judging as a member of a panel of three or more adjudicators at a championship event.

The above are examples of some of the typical rules.

What it's all about: a range of world championship trophies.

CHAPTER 7

OPPORTUNITIES AFTER COMPETITION

There was still no likelihood that we could make a living from dance. We were doing it because we loved it. We realized how full we felt; we were surrounded by music and dancing and joy.

Alvin Ailey

Most participants in Irish dancing start their dancing as a hobby or a sporting activity. A large number do not progress much further than this, and just continue their dancing activities very much as a social interest. The more ambitious performers enter the competition world, and a selected few are good enough to become world champions, although even at this highest level the pastime still remains primarily an amateur activity. However, for the highly motivated and dedicated dancer there are numerous opportunities to further their working careers, either academically or in the performing arts in a number of different ways. In addition, some will embark on a teaching career, and even go on to open their own dance school.

Furthermore, there are many other roles within and associated with the dance business that contribute towards the performing arts scene. These professional opportunities offer a dancer the prospect of significant financial rewards and a lasting, satisfying working life, an exciting career, or something they just love doing.

For those who remain amateurs, and with the increasing numbers of dancers worldwide, there has been a significant increase in extra-mural activities for the enthusiast to enjoy. Most of these are available and advertised in the social media outlets referred to earlier.

This chapter identifies and discusses a number of the more interesting opportunities potentially available to talented Irish dancers in the world today.

EDUCATION

Opportunities in Further Education

Several universities around the world offer degrees in Irish dance and music, or in dance and music as separate entities. These courses generate job positions such as lecturer, teacher's assistant, or administratively as a course director or department coordinator. There are many opportunities to share Irish dance with eager scholars.

One of the largest and best-known institutions that offers a wide range of graduate and post-graduate courses is the University of Limerick.[26] Built beside the River Shannon near the city of Limerick in Ireland, the university houses 'The World Academy of Irish Music and Dance', where it is now possible to read for a BA or MA in Irish dancing, and even to research for a PhD in a dance-related project. Students are based in the Irish World Academy Building, which has world-class facilities and is equipped to the highest standards with cutting edge performance and rehearsal spaces and technological infrastructure. Tuition is provided by a faculty of excellent performers and academics, as well as industry professionals and international guest artists and researchers. Some of the content of the courses available at Limerick[27] is summarized below.

OPPOSITE: **Cast of Lord of the Dance – show-dancing job opportunities.**

The Irish Dance BA Degree

The Irish Dance BA degree at UoL[27] is a three- or four-year, full-time undergraduate programme designed to develop dance skills and knowledge, as well as to encourage other forms of musical and artistic expression. Students spend extensive studio time developing technique and repertoires in the dance studios at the academy. They are also encouraged to develop knowledge and enquiry around their own discipline and genre. They are introduced to other performance practices and traditions in order to gain new insights into the worlds of dance and the performing arts. They also study a number of vocationally focused modules aimed at allowing students to translate artistic and scholarly creativity into a fulfilling career.

The programme prepares the graduate for many different career paths, including professional performance, further study and research, work in cultural institutions, media-related posts, archival work and performance production, all in entrepreneurial ways.

The Irish Dance Studies MA Degree

The Irish Dance Studies MA degree at UoL is a one-year, full-time taught postgraduate programme. It is unique in that it is the only programme of its type at any university in the world. It considers Irish dance practices and related idioms within cultural, historical and practice-based perspectives. Students on the programme critically engage with relevant literature and dance practices, and undertake field research in a relevant Irish dance study of their choice. The aim of the programme is to provide students with contextual and historical dance notation, and embodied knowledge relating to different Irish dance practices. It also provides an invaluable foundation for those wishing to pursue dance research to doctorate level.

PhD Research

The Irish World Academy is also a major international centre for PhD and Master degree research across a broad range of academic disciplines, focusing on music and dance, but not exclusively so. Research students work with supervisors

Details of The Irish World Academy of Music and Dance.

A piece choreographed by Fernanda Faez from Brazil, who was reading for her MA at UoL in 2021, with financial support from The Marie Duffy Foundation.

across the academy – at times, supervisory input from across the university and wider afield is sought. There are usually around forty-five research students at the academy at any one time, and the majority of these are undertaking PhDs with traditional outputs such as a thesis. The academy provides a comprehensive support infrastructure for research students, including the following:

- Access to seminars and other research-focused events and classes.
- Funding opportunities.
- Teaching opportunities.
- Performance opportunities.
- Financial support for conferences.

These are provided in addition to the many supports and opportunities for professional development offered by the university through the Graduate School. Research degrees are usually developed with a potential supervisor who is a member of the academic faculty. Further details on the full range of courses and opportunities available at UoL can be found on their website.[27]

BECOME A DANCE TEACHER

Not surprisingly, becoming a dance teacher is perhaps one of the most popular career choices for dancers. With the relevant qualification, teachers can teach Irish dance in a studio, in Irish dance schools and in public schools. This choice also allows the dancer to remain physically active while sharing their knowledge with others. It helps to know which age group you want to teach, as some will require extra training or college degrees.

This is a great option, which helps extend a dancing career. A recommended route would be to study for a TCRG or TMRF or other certification, and become a fully qualified Irish dance teacher. (*See* Chapter 6 for full details on the syllabus for the An Coimisiún qualification.) In the longer term the opportunity of opening your own dance school becomes a realistic option.

OPPORTUNITIES IN SHOW DANCING

Following on from the outstanding success of the Riverdance presentation at the interval of The Eurovision Song Competition held in Ireland in 1994, a large number of show dance opportunities became available. Initially two major shows started – The Riverdance Show itself, and following Michael Flatley's break with Riverdance, his own show Lord of the Dance. A significant number of new, albeit smaller shows followed as they became increasingly more popular throughout the world.

A typical show at this level employs around forty dancers in a troupe, and even more as in some of Michael Flatley's productions such as Feet of Flames, with as many as a hundred dancers performing. By early 2010, with a number of different troupes touring all parts of the globe simultaneously, as many as 400 dancers could be actively performing from these two shows alone. At its peak Lord of the Dance had four troupes touring round the globe at the same time.

The undoubted and enduring popularity of Irish show dancing continues, and a number of other show companies have emerged, further raising the number of professional dancers participating at any one point in time. Whilst offering the successful dancers a lucrative living, these companies also provide the opportunity of travelling around the world.

Over the last twenty-five years Irish dance shows have performed on every continent and in many countries. They perform in a large range of venues, from small theatres to large arenas such as the O2 and Wembley in London, in front of audiences of up to 15,000 people for an individual performance – Lord of the Dance performed at a football stadium in Budapest in front of an audience of 80,000.

Whilst the numbers involved today are marginally fewer, show dancing still offers the talented dancer an exciting and fulfilling career opportunity for a number of years.

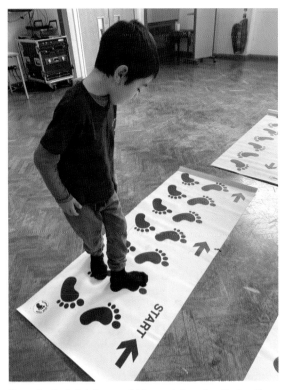

Use of a helpful dance aid to assist and optimize the dance teaching process.

Use of the dance aid to learn the basic sidestep.

Use of the dance aid to learn how to turn out the feet.

Use of the dance aid for more basic foot placements.

A female lead dancer: Bernadette Flynn as Saoirse in Lord of the Dance.

A female lead dancer: Ciara Sexton as Morrighan in Lord of the Dance.

A female ensemble in Celtic Dreams in Lord of the Dance.

A male lead dancer: Tom Cunningham as Don Dorcha in Lord of the Dance.

Victory for the Dark Lord.

A male ensemble of the warlords versus warriors in 'Nightmare' from Lord of the Dance.

OPPORTUNITIES IN WORKSHOPS AND SEMINARS

There has also been an increase in the number of workshops, dance camps and seminars available for dancers to join. Workshops are usually, although not exclusively, organized during the summer holidays, and can last for a day or a week and in some cases even longer. Seminars are held throughout the year and usually at weekends. Typically they concentrate on a specific topic, such as new choreography for set dances, or exercising and fitness; they may also focus on subjects such as exam preparation or an introduction to show dancing. Opportunities there fore arise for employment either as an instructor/ lecturer or as a participant. Summer camps have also become increasingly popular.

OTHER POTENTIAL JOB OPPORTUNITIES

There are many factors involved in the world of Irish dance, and a range of alternative, but related, job opportunities potentially exist for worthwhile future careers. A very useful source of information is One Dance UK.[28] Just take a little time to think about all your skills and activities involved in the various facets of Irish dancing, and look for creative ways to develop those with your favourite parts of Irish dance. A number of additional potential job opportunities for an Irish dancer are described below.

Choreography

Opportunities exist for the development and commercialization of your own individual innovative work, or for the establishment of your own dance company. Consider working with local dance and theatre groups who may be interested in hiring a choreographer for their plays or musicals. In addition, large-scale entertainment companies may need choreographers for corporate or commercial work.

Costume Design

As a dancer you will have been surrounded by costumes throughout your dancing career, and

Innovative choreography – 'I'm Late, I'm Late' by Ella Owens.

Innovative choreography – 'Taxi' by Ella Owens.

you will know what feels good to dance or practise in. With this advantage, you can create costumes, dancewear or clothing that is designed to be moved in or to move well with the body! If you are passionate about designing your own gear, you could even start your own line. The internet has paved the way for a booming self-employment market for dressmaking. Teaching yourself how to sew and creating your own costumes could lead you into a new business. Alternatively use these skills to obtain work in the costume department of a dance company. There are entire teams behind many dress brands and positions, from designers, to marketers, to webmasters and accountants, all involved in making dance costumes happen worldwide.

Initial sketch for a dress design.

Another sketch for a dress design.

Hair and Make-Up Styling

As well as dress, a key part of the competition world is hair and make-up presentation. With the increasing number of feiseanna, dance competitions and competitors, there are more and more opportunities for dancers who have acquired styling skills for both wig selection and fitting, and make-up application, to pursue a worthwhile career. A dance competition can last the best part of the day, and dancers are using professional help with both of these activities. Increasing specialist practitioners are setting up facilities at all the major events, and opportunities exist to establish one's own business in these and complementary fields.

Dance Photography and Videographing

As a dancer you already have an awareness of movement, so if you are attracted by the photography world, you will be able to predict great photo moments or video framing. Dancers and choreographers often have a great eye for creating imagery – after all, dance is essentially creating images with our bodies. There are also opportunities to photograph

for the shows. Whether you strike out on your own as a freelance photographer, or you spend time as an apprentice with an established photographer, if you enjoy being behind a camera this may be a career for you. Bear in mind, however, that there are strict rules relating to child protection, copyright and children's rights, and you would need to familiarize yourself with these.

Arts Administration and Show Management

Jobs exist in dance companies and theatres in the administrative area. Experience in the dance world provides a thorough understanding of the arts in general, and making the transition to a desk job is a good option to stay involved in the dancing arena if you desire a less physically active career. These can be great positions for those who can also organize budgetary finances, schedule meetings, rehearsals or shows, organize fundraisers, and support the management of the company. A range of other opportunities is also possible in areas such as set design and construction, lighting, sound control, wardrobe and dressing, stage and tour management, and public relations.

Lord of the Dance cast members preparing for the show in the make-up area.

Original hand-drawn picture of a céilí champion team by Fionnuala Conway.

Yoga or Pilates Teaching

Yoga and Pilates are not only great conditioning activities for dancers, they also make wonderful second careers and offer the potential for additional income for part- and full-time dancers. There are many similarities between the execution of dance and these activities. Several types of training course are available to qualify for teaching both dance and yoga, and Pilates. Most gyms and studios will require this in-depth training in order for someone to teach. Opportunities also exist to teach private lessons or at corporate offices.

Marketing for Dancers

Work in the marketing field could entail designing and maintaining web pages, designing flyers and other promotional materials, promoting events through social media, and more. Graphic design work may require additional training, which can be received through on-line courses, community classes, or attending college to obtain a degree or an equivalent qualification. There are many businesses within Irish dance that have to find a way to advertise what they offer. Marketing can fit many different skill sets. As a graphic designer you could work on the logos and advertisement art for shows, bands or other dance brands. Or there is web design, or branding, or helping a show, product, or company determine its name or identity, and even placing advertisements in brochures, newspapers and so on.

Physiotherapy, Nutrition, Physical Fitness

Every dancer knows their body very well. Those who have had extensive training, such as that demanded by a college degree programme, probably have a wide range of nutritional, anatomical and kinesiology knowledge. Injuries in dance are unfortunately common: you may have experienced some yourself and have received physical therapy. This can be an excellent and lucrative field for a dancer to enter.

The ability to relate to a dancer and to understand the dancer's body offers many opportunities as a physical therapist, nutritionist or fitness instructor. In addition there are potential vacancies working in gyms as personal trainers.

Media and Journalism

Are you a writer? Do you love asking questions or telling stories? Publications such as *Irish Dance* magazine and *Dance* magazine are great platforms to aim for. Many of these offer internships, and if articles are not your speciality, there are always sales, fact checking, web design, multimedia content editing and more – all with dance as the core focus.

IN CONCLUSION

These are just a few ideas on how you can either extend your dance career, or make the transition into a new field. When searching for a new job, be sure to think about all the great skills and ideas that dance has provided you, such as discipline, punctuality, dedication, creativity, kinesthetics awareness and more. Know that your drive to succeed does not have to stop with dance, but these many wonderful qualities will help you to open new doors, build new bridges, and have a successful and happy life, no matter what you do.

Imagination offers endless opportunities – outside the box.

CHAPTER 8

CHOREOGRAPHY

To be creative means to be in love with life. You can be creative only if you love life enough that you want to enhance its beauty, you want to bring a little more music to it, a little more dance to it.

Osho

WHAT IS CHOREOGRAPHY?

Choreography is the art of creating a dance routine or new steps by grouping together and organizing different dance moves into sequences and patterns that can be performed to a specific song or melody.

There are two types of choreography: improvisation or planned choreography. Improvisation is where dancers have a general guideline but can then interpret some of the movements or steps themselves. Planned choreography is dictated to dancers in specific detail. Choreographers create original dance steps and put together moves in sequence for a dance routine, and develop new interpretations of existing dances. They teach complex dance movements and sometimes work with performers who are untrained dancers.

HOW TO CHOREOGRAPH A DANCE

Choreographing a dance movement or steps requires creativity, patience and hard work. It usually takes at least two to three days, and often longer, to choreograph a four-minute dance, depending on the dance type and the choreographer. The key elements of dance choreography, common to all genres, are body, action, space, time and energy. Being able to identify and understand these core characteristics will help you, as choreographer, to convey your message through movement. However, it is important to remember that before piecing together the perfect routine, let the music and genre inspire you.

Inspiration

Initially spend some time thinking about and developing the routine. What is the message or story you wish to get across, or mood to convey? Look for inspiration from other performers and routines. Think about the judges, the audience, the venues and the type of story you will be using. Select the dance style you wish to use, choose the music, and decide on the number of dancers you are going to use.

Continually familiarize yourself with the music: break it down into sections and identify the potential energy levels and rhythms of each section. Consider the rise and fall and the light and shade of the music. Initially create a list of steps, moves and sequences that are not only genre appropriate, but also fit the music. Regularly review progress and make changes when they become apparent, and use this inspiration time wisely.

Develop Movement

Start the detailed preparation of the routine. Experiment with different steps, moves and sequences, and combine them to create a number of sections

Lively, colourful, innovative figure-dance movement.

specific to the music. Interpret the music through your dancers' movement and facial expressions. Ensure the individual dance sections are seamlessly linked and unify the routine by creating transitions for dancers to move from section to section.

Use of Costumes and Props

Whenever possible use props, but only to complement and enhance the movement. Costumes, particularly in Irish dancing, will show off the choreography, and sounds can also enhance the routine.

Finally, Choreograph your Routine

Once all the preparatory work has been completed, write out the routine in advance of the first rehearsal. Ensure that all the details of the steps and transitions are listed as necessary. Use your own language and notations, and in particular deal with complex passages, so you can spend additional time explaining and demonstrating them.

Preparation for 'The First Night'

'Practice makes Perfect'

The well-known saying 'practice makes perfect' is undoubtedly true. Remember to practise the routine over and over again until all the dancers are not only competent with the dance steps but also brimming with confidence. Patience is essential, as dancers develop and learn at different paces. Teach and rehearse them to learn the dance and understand how to interpret your vision. Always lead from the front, remain positive, but stay flexible and responsive to altering your choreography if something is not working. Seek and accept input from others, particularly your dance captains and lead dancers.

Staging

Staging is particularly important in a routine that includes a number of dancers, such as a figure dance, a dance drama or a show number. You will need to rehearse the routine as many times as the schedule will allow on the stage where you will be performing. Decide how and where the dancers will enter and exit the stage. Mark up the stage with lines and spots on the floor in the positions where the dancers should be at various points in the dance, and alter the transitions as necessary to facilitate this. It is important to step away from the stage and view your creation from various positions

'Routine choreography, but practice makes perfect.'

in the auditorium. Check the sight lines and make sure that all the dancers can be clearly seen from all positions, and that none are obstructed by the building or props.

Revise your Choreography

After several rehearsals you will need to review the performance with the dance troupe. Don't be afraid to revise the choreography. Perfect and optimize the steps and transitions. Make notes of the areas where the dancers could improve their dance, and equally important, be sure that they are transmitting the emotion you wish to communicate. Work with the dancers, make the necessary changes, and then hold a dress rehearsal before the opening night.

The foregoing sections relate to dance choreography in general and are applicable for most dance genres. The next few paragraphs investigate choreography in the different forms of Irish dance, as each category has its own rules and guidelines. Some have a lot more scope and freedom than others, not only in steps and movements but also in costuming and props.

CHOREOGRAPHY IN SOLO IRISH DANCING

Choreography for a teacher or dancer mainly starts after the beginner status has been successfully completed. It is fairly standardized up to that point, but as the dancer progresses through the grades to advanced championship standard it becomes much more complex, difficult and syncopated. These days the scope for innovation is quite wide and varied, although the basic rules and regulations, especially in competitions and major championships, must still be observed. You need to check with your organization for their interpretations, as these can vary.

When choreographing a solo dance and steps the dancer is generally given a set number of bars that have to be completed and a specific range of metronomic speeds to dance to. Each step is usually performed on the right and left foot. The choreography should not affect the dancer's posture/carriage, which means that a straight line from head to toe must be maintained. No movement should affect any part of their posture – so when they jump or leap they must not lean forwards or backwards or lift or

Dancer leaping for joy and expressing freedom to move away from the restraints of traditional Irish dance.

bend the arms from their side. They must maintain the correct line at all times. In a light shoe routine, the dancer should land lightly on the toes or high on the ball of the foot without dropping the heels on landing or making a sound as they land, such as a thud. In a heavy shoe they should also land lightly with just the sound of their beat, not a thud, and neither should they drop the heels to clip off the floor.

The following are some guidelines regarding dos and don'ts when choreographing steps or set dances:

- Take account of the music and speed.
- Don't overcrowd or overload the routine: this happens quite often, especially in heavy shoe dancing and slow set dances, in particular when you over-syncopate. The material should fit the music comfortably and allow the dancer to perform it with ease, without stress or strain, and without it affecting their carriage, no matter how much effort they put in – if it's too packed it will not fit or flow.
- There is a beat (the dancers' term for the sound they are making) for every note (of music), and a note for every beat, and it is important to put the beats on the right note. Even if the routine is very syncopated and off beat, it must still be in time. Sometimes it is difficult for the teacher or dancer to understand this. Saying that 'it's off the beat' is no excuse or argument, as it must still *fit* and be in time.
- Two other important facts in choreography are the rise and fall of the music, and light and shade. Listen to the music and interpret it into the sound and rhythm of the step. Is there a story to the tune, or does it originate in a certain or special place, year or century? Especially in set dances, many of their names help interpret the music, in particular dances such as Kilkenny Races.
- In some of today's choreographies, the choreographer is too obsessed with the most popular 'tricks' of the season, instead of listening to and interpreting the music. The same choreography is repeated, especially in heavy shoe and set dance rounds, whether it's 6/8 or 4/4, or 2/4: it is transcribed from jig to hornpipe by slowing the speed to fit the piece, rather than choreographing to the music itself. There is a school of thought that a 4/4 piece should not be slowed down to a metronomic speed of 76, taking it into jig time and rhythm. However, this is an argument for another day.
- In solo choreography the dancer should give a strong performance – not aggressive, but easy on the eye.

Two excellent examples of developing the music to the story, and the subsequent basic choreographing of the routine to the music, are given at the end of Chapter 4 in the solo set dances The Vanishing Lake and The Charlady.

CHOREOGRAPHY IN IRISH FIGURE DANCING

As the World Irish Dancing Championships grew from its inception to what it is today, it became more popular, and so did the interest in, and the number of people experimenting with, figure choreography.

'Flying high over Glasgow': transition from traditional dancing to modern dynamic Irish dance.

In those early days it went under the heading of 'Figure Dancing Championships', and the initial rules were fairly simple and straightforward:

- The number of dancers in the dance could be up to sixteen.
- Only dance steps used in ceílí dancing, such as the threes and sevens and rising step, could be used.
- The dance would have been danced either in reel time or jig time from start to finish, and only Irish music was permitted.
- The routine had to interpret an Irish historic theme or event.

As the competition became more popular, the creations and choreography became more complex and intricate. In addition, the innovators developed very beautiful and graceful routines depicting historical events or places throughout Ireland. One could follow the theme and music by the portrayal of the dancers and the choreography. Also, as the competition grew in popularity, entry numbers increased dramatically. Entries were now coming from further afield than just Ireland, England, Scotland and Wales, including from across the Atlantic from the USA and Canada, and further still, Australia. Figure dancing became the highlight of the event, and as the competition grew, so did the audiences, and so did the creativity. This also fuelled imaginations in a number of areas such as the design of costumes, the range of dances, more innovations in steps and hand movements, and the introduction of props.

As the routines became more varied, CLRG felt it necessary to review this escalation, and held

Inis Ealga, World Champion figure-dance team from the 1980s.

major discussions as to how to control the development of this dance form – essentially, whether such innovations should be allowed to continue, or whether tighter controls and regulations should be adopted. After much debate it was decided that there was actually room for both, but to divide them into two categories, one for figure dancing, with the same stipulations as originally introduced, and a new breakout section called dance drama. This would have a much wider scope regarding choreography, footwork and steps, more embellished arm and body movements, and more props allowed. (For further information *see* the dance drama choreography section below.)

So figure dancing became known as figure choreography, and continued to flourish, with beautiful performances and storytelling masterpieces with intricate designs. Then after some time it took off in a different direction once again. It became faster moving, dances continuing with sevens but with very few threes, and it moved more in lines, regularly forming diagonal movements that went in the same or different directions across and up and down the stage. Arm movements became more syncopated, and were often performed individually rather than linked together as before. Costumes became more in line with the theme of the dance, with more features such as headgear, which added to the presentation and overall effect.

The dancing movements and steps then came under further criticism and attack for moving too far away from the rules, especially when more solo steps with leaps and twirls, spins and elevated pieces were introduced and the over-use of 'continuous sevens' without 'threes'. In addition, basic steps such as variations of the rising step from Ár Rincí Céilí were not being used enough, and movements such as cartwheels or handstands were not allowed. Future budding figure choreographers must ensure that their music selection is Irish and not controversial, otherwise they may be disqualified – although there is a much wider choice available to choose from now. Voice-overs during the performance are not permitted.

As in solo choreography, do not overload or overcrowd the routine – less is more. It should be easy on the eye, and the audience should be able to understand and see and follow the story easily. You need to have a strong opening, middle and end.

Finally, carefully read and adhere to the rules and regulations of the organization you belong to, as these do vary. Remember these are the guidelines that the adjudicators are given to judge under and adhere to. Below are some useful tips that are relevant for both solo and team choreography:

- Listen to the music over and over again and visualize it – the steps, the movements and the dancers – until you have a real feel for your creation.
- Map the stage – make a stage plan, navigating and utilizing as much of the stage as possible. Break down the dance/step into sections – draw out the stage and decide where each part will go. Colour code it, and when you have finished, check the pattern to see if there are empty spaces to fill.
- For solo choreography ensure the choreography allows your dancer to 'visit' all the judges. There is no point in dancing to empty spaces with judges straining their necks trying to see – they just lose interest. Remember you are there to entertain them, and the performance must keep them engaged and they must feel it is specifically for them.

Action shot from a performance by Edward Searle and Byron Tuttle, The Academy, USA World Champions 2019 in figure dance.

- Performance is paramount: the dancers' performance should not be aggressive, but should be easy on the eye. A smile is worth a thousand steps. Lead from the front and be positive, flexible and responsive.

CHOREOGRAPHY IN IRISH DANCING DANCE DRAMAS

As discussed in the above section, when figure dance choreography started to stray away from the set down rules for steps, arms, movements and props and become more dramatic, it was decided to create another category in competition that could embrace such developments. Hence the dance drama category was added to the programme of the World Championships. It started with two age groups, under sixteen and over sixteen, but at some point it went to being over sixteen only.

Some of the rules from the figure dance section are carried over, such as, it must be an Irish theme or event. The music rule is slightly different in that it must still be Irish, but there is an allowance for music of other influences to be used very briefly if it is connected to the dance, the theme and the storyline. The number of bars also needs to be checked to see if the tune length is acceptable. The music for both the dance drama and figure dance competition must be submitted in advance to be checked. The following are some of the key rules for dance dramas:

- Up to twenty dancers are allowed to participate in a dance drama, whereas in the figure dance, no more than sixteen can participate in a team.
- In the figure dance they have to remain on stage from start to finish, whereas in the dance drama they may enter and exit the stage at various times as in a play, according to the story being portrayed.
- There is more flexibility allowed in the field of costumes. Costumes suitable to the storyline, the event, the place, the era and the country may be used and even changed, time permitting during the performance.
- Another big difference in this category is that props are allowed. In the early days these were simple and uncomplicated. The competition has now grown and developed into a very professional and sophisticated production, and this has brought with it more sophisticated sets, lighting and costumes. Location is not a restraint: entries are global, and the transporting of very elaborate and cumbersome sets does not seem to lower the enthusiasm or the entry.
- As a choreographer you have more flexibility – you are not so restricted in the steps or footwork. Light shoe, heavy shoe and/or a combination of the two can be used. Neither are you restricted to

Figure-dance show style – the closing of 'Siamsa' in Lord of the Dance.

Inis Ealga Senior World Champion dance drama in the 1970s: 'The story of St Patrick.'

the basic ceílí steps – solo steps and variations thereof are acceptable.

- Similarly arm and body movements relating to the story are used, likewise the drama and acting all become an essential part of the production.

In competition, marks are allotted separately to all these sections, along with the overall impact of the presentation. It is important to consider these factors when choreographing. Remember, it's a drama told through dance, music and mime, with no voice-over permitted. In addition, the presentation must finish within the time allocated for the performance – this applies to both dance drama and figure dancing and is strictly adhered to. Because of dance drama's popularity at the World Championships it is usually a stand-alone event with a large demand for tickets.

Key points for a good dance drama production include the following:

- Read the rules and specifications and adhere to them.
- Research the story, and explore how it can be adapted to be a creative musical and dance production – how much impact can be produced. Consider the highs and lows, light and shade, rise and fall, and the variety of music it lends itself to. Be it a serious historical event or a fun production, the engagement of the audience and adjudicators is your aim.

'In the land of choro' ('Na terra do choro'): 'choro' is a kind of Brazilian music from the south-east of Brazil. It was a precursor of samba music. The dancers are from Banana Broadway, São Paulo, Brazil.

- Choose the music wisely – and check copyright, it may be necessary to obtain approval to use it. Check that it is suitable and allowable for the competition you are entering.
- Keep to the allotted time, including the time needed to set up and clear the stage.
- Check the size and suitability of the stage for the props and the number of dancers in the routine. Check the lighting and other production factors such as sightlines, entrances and exits.
- Ensure that the music recording is of a good sound quality and production. Play it beforehand and check sound levels.

2007: 'Pulsation' ('Pulsação'): the choreography is based on samba characters 'mestre-sala' and 'porta-bandeira', which are very elegant and have a vertical posture. The choreography incorporates samba movements to Irish dance. The dancers are from Banana Broadway, São Paulo, Brazil.

- For the choreography, follow all the points at the beginning of this chapter and give your creativity free rein. Remember, you have much more freedom to push the boundaries, and are subject to fewer restrictions. Take advantage of this to make it your most outstanding choreography to date.

CHOREOGRAPHY IN IRISH DANCE SHOWS

In Dublin in 1994 at the Eurovision Song Contest, Michael Flatley burst on to the stage to the drums of Bill Whelan's music: it was the seven-minute interval piece, and at the end the audience exploded. The routine grabbed the headlines that year, and changed the face of Irish dancing for ever. Michael Flatley, with his partner Jean Butler and a troupe of Irish dancers, took both the place and the world by storm: Irish dancing in its own unique beautiful style of rhythm and grace, now had another dimension: it was *sexy*. As we know, traditionally Irish dancing is performed with the arms down by the side of the body, the upper part of the body remaining still and seamless – but this changed everything.

Out of this interval piece was born Riverdance, followed very quickly by Lord of the Dance, created by Michael Flatley. The success of these two shows encouraged the arrival of other smaller shows, thus giving Irish dancers a dancing career after competition,

and opening up many more avenues and careers for those involved in the genre (*see* Chapter 7).

Dancing and choreography changed dramatically, as the competition rules and the rules of the various organizations didn't apply. Total freedom of movement, and arms down by the sides of the body disappeared (in shows, that is), and the use of upper body movements became part of the integral choreography. There was no right or wrong way: it was Michael Flatley's way. Innovation had no bounds or boundaries, creativity flowed, and with it a new artistic Irish dance form took to the stage, not only with arm and body movements, but facial expressions depicting the physical movements, and mesmerizing rhythms and acapella footwork unseen and unheard before, became the new norm.

This innovative choreography brought many changes. Take upper body and arm movements, for instance – it seemed to come easily and naturally for Michael Flatley to use his arms as he danced to express himself, having bolted on to the stage like thunder and lightning: it was his own style. If you look at his performances or photographs you will see how developed his upper body and muscle tone is.

For males wishing to develop this style it is necessary to develop upper body strength and muscle tone: it doesn't come overnight. It takes months of training commitment and discipline, going to the gym, possibly engaging with a personal trainer at least to get started and to work on the right muscle

Modern female group choreography in 'Breakout', led by Bernadette Flynn.

groups. Then it's up to the individual to maintain this body shape and fitness. The males in the show do this all the time, even on tour: they have weights and other equipment that goes on tour with them, and they have a regular routine and training cycle that they have to follow strictly.

Then it is necessary to transmit the shapes and movements into the dance routine, whether this involves movements for the 'good' character 'the lord' or for the 'villain' Don Dorcha, who has more aggressive and attacking movements and shapes. Both these male lead roles bring out the strong masculinity of the dance and the characters, and the males in the troupe therefore need to follow a routine and pattern of training to maintain their stamina, physicality and dancing fitness. To do so a good size space – a studio with mirrors – is imperative for drilling, training and maintenance.

The female roles in the show also demand very rigid training in both physical fitness, body tone and dance. Going to the gym frequently and engaging a personal trainer if possible is a step in the right direction. Irish dance today is quite athletic, and particularly in shows, so being physically fit is paramount, along with body and muscle tone and stamina.

The female show style brings out the femininity and sexiness of the roles, be it either as the 'good' girl or the 'bad' girl. The 'good' side calls for a deli-

cate, graceful demure, quite balletic in style and easy on the eye, and the choreography should portray this. Body and arm movements need to be slow and graceful, especially as they extend. Facial expression should show joy and happiness or sadness. On the other hand the 'bad' girl, or vixen, needs to portray a smouldering sexiness or a sexiness with rage and control, with Spanish and Latin American influences – unlike the tango, although it does have rise and fall. It is therefore possibly best suited to 4/4 time. Choreographing a solo for this type of character should be fast moving, exciting, with plenty of elevation, leaps intertwined with spins in the air or on the floor, arms well extended as the dancer takes flight, with smouldering eyes and facial expression. A very good example and portrayal of this is the character Morrighan, the temptress in Lord of the Dance.

Whichever side you wish to portray, plenty of space is needed for movement, and mirrors are useful for work and practice.

When choreographing for a group or for a solo you may find that is it difficult to start with using the arms, especially if you have been competing in Irish dance for a long time with the arms straight down and still. It works well to get the girls to loosen up and become less rigid by playing music such as a slip jig. Get all girls up on the floor together, moving in different directions, independently of each other,

Bernadette Flynn in Celtic Dreams from Lord of the Dance, depicting grace, femininity and elegance.

In contrast, Ciara Sexton as the temptress Morrighan portrays a smouldering sexiness.

dancing round 'freestyle' using body and arms with their own interpretation of and feel for the music. Dancing continuously until the music finishes, and after a couple of rounds of this, they move more loosely and freely, developing their own style. Then direct and choreograph a piece for them or yourself. This is very stimulating for all, and any self-consciousness in using the body and arms soon vanishes. If you are choreographing a 'vixen' role do a similar exercise with faster music, such as reel music in 4/4 time.

A frequently asked question by budding choreographers is 'Which comes first, the music or the choreography?' Well, in shows especially this varies. In competitions the music is already composed, and you choreograph to it accordingly. In shows, especially in the creation of a new show, the music and dance are composed simultaneously. Usually the storyline and plot come first, and these are developed and expanded by the producer and director as time passes. The composer along with the producer and director and choreographers take on the musicality and artistic look. Then the music theme, along with new ideas, is discussed and tried.

At times the composer prepares music for a certain scene, and from there the choreographer works on its interpretation into dance. On other occasions the director and/or choreographer speak with the composer and discuss ideas of movement or rhythms, and the music follows. It is usually the whole artistic team in collaboration that brings a successful show to its fruition.

Overall, choreography in all its various forms is the most challenging, exciting, fulfilling and rewarding activity in Irish dancing. It can be summarized by the quote already given at the beginning of Chapter 4 by Torron-Lee Dewar:

Every dance you make belongs to you. It is part of your collection. When you think of it like that, you'll want to make your next routine the best you've ever made.

Torron-Lee Dewar

The dances in this party are the 'quadrilhas', originating in European quadrilles. This choreography describes traditional céilís, danced with music, costumes and narration typical of the Brazilian festival 'Céilí Junina'. The dancers are from Banana Broadway, São Paulo, Brazil.

CHAPTER 9

MENTAL AND PHYSICAL FITNESS, AND HEALTH AND SAFETY

The only way to make sense out of change is to plunge into it, move with it, and join the dance.
Alan W. Watts

In recent years, complementary factors relating to the physical and mental aspects of the Irish dancer have become increasingly important. In addition, in recent decades many other health and safety matters and issues have emerged, and new legislation has become mandatory in many areas relevant to the management of Irish dance teaching. This section will first discuss some of the latest thinking in these non-dancing areas, which is equally relevant and important to both the beginner and the championship dancer. It will explore some of the new thinking on the development of the dancer's body and mind, and will introduce the SAP concept as a route to success. Secondly, it will examine in some detail the vitally important areas of diet and exercise. Finally it will highlight the major health and safety factors and issues as they relate to the management of Irish dance schools and the teaching and care of young dancers.

THE SAP PROGRAMME

In 2013, at a seminar held at the University of Limerick, the Marie Duffy Foundation introduced the SAP programme as a concept to fully embrace the essential factors of body, heart and soul. The object of the programme is to help nurture and strengthen the knowledge and expertise required to be successful in today's modern environment. So, what is SAP?

SAP stands for Strength, Agility and Preparation, which are the three core attributes considered a necessity for success in the modern Irish dance world. In a little more detail, the main ingredients of these key factors can be summarized as follows:

- Strength: maximal development in mind, body and character.
- Agility: the ability to think fast, adapt quickly and have a body fit for purpose.
- Preparation: to be fully prepared in knowledge, mindset, nutrition and physicality.

So, what does this mean in practice? The next few paragraphs will explain and explore in more detail some of the thinking behind the SAP concept.

STRENGTH

One of the leading pioneers and practitioners in this field of healthcare is Michael O'Doherty, based in Co. Clare in Ireland. Michael founded Plexus Health Care, he was the co-founder of a therapy called Plexus Bio Energy, and has many years' experience in advising people how to live a healthy life. He passionately believes that your body is *your* business because only *you* can control which thoughts, feelings and beliefs you allow into your brain. These thoughts, beliefs and feelings have been scientifically proven to significantly affect every cell in your body. We are indebted to Michael for his contribution to the Strength part of our SAP programme, the key factors of which are highlighted below.[25]

Michael O'Doherty guiding a group of Irish dancers along the road to success.

Achieving Your True Potential

The first part of understanding body, heart and soul is how to avoid burnout. First, use your mindset, commitment and sacrifice to move your focus from winning to preparation. It is often said that you have to be born gifted to be successful in business or sport, or to be a world champion dancer or teacher, and unfortunately many people believe this to be true. In reality, however, nothing can be further from the truth. We are all born with the ability to achieve whatever we want in life, and while some may have to work harder than others, the only person who prevents you from making it to the top is *you.*

The next sections can help you gain an insight into, and equip you with some of the skills that will enable you to achieve your true potential. The way the mind works affects the body in many ways, and if you can use your mind and emotions to have the edge, you will be a winner and will realize your future dreams. Strength, agility and preparation will prepare you for your pathway to success, but at the end of the day the fundamentals to this pathway will be your level of commitment, belief and sacrifice. The road map to success helps you to access your hidden potential, and if you are willing to embrace these principles of how the human being functions you can be on top of the world.

Visualization: the Power of Your Mind

We all have the ability to shape our own futures if we are willing to take the steps to rediscover our power. A lot is written about the law of attraction, but you also need to focus on the law of creation by using your mind to create the person you need and want to be. Everything begins with an image, and people have no problem seeing negative things happening to them but not so readily the positive things. Often people find it very hard to practise visualizing being positive – for example, when you woke up this morning, how did you see your day shaping up: did you see yourself lacking energy, experiencing stress, pain and anxiety, filled with fear and worry?

Well, that is visualization, and what you are seeing, perceiving, feeling and thinking is creating your day and your world. But do you realize the damage you are potentially causing to your health and body by doing this, when all you need do is take that same energy and use it to achieve the opposite?

People who make it to the top in all walks of life have one common thread running through them, and that is, they have developed their mind in ways whereby they can create the life of their choosing. Their ability to be dynamic and open to change enables them to grow and develop through every experience.

Never begin a new project unless you have prepared correctly, and it is through that preparation you can achieve success. Whether it be in health, business, sport or dancing, your ability to visualize creatively by engaging in a daily routine, by using your mind to create whatever it is you would like to happen, will determine the outcome. It often does not seem that way, but somewhere out of the universe or as we sometimes say 'out of the blue', something happens and it all comes together. This only happens to those who are willing to open up to all possibilities and remain positive. As Nelson Mandela said, 'It is not our darkness we fear, but our light.'

The use of functional MRI scans has shown that when professional athletes were asked to visualize themselves running a marathon while they were in a sitting position, their brain fired the muscle fibres associated to the event, as if they were really running that marathon. Visualization is a very powerful tool to use in our daily lives to achieve whatever we want to achieve and more, and the more we need to embrace it.

The Creative Visualization Process

The following are some simple steps that will help you achieve your goals using your mind, and though doubts will emerge from time to time, do stay with it. You have nothing to fear because you are the only person who can stop you from being the best at whatever you do.

The first step is to learn to relax your body and clear your mind.

The second step is to practise creative visualization by learning to imagine your intended outcome. Your imagination is the basis of your thoughts and feelings. Imagine your ideal world in the present moment, bring your images to life as if watching a movie, concentrate your thoughts with laser-like precision, and indulge all your senses.

The third step is to really feel as if you had already what you would like to have. Sense the emotion of joy, love and happiness in the present physical moment.

The fourth step in the creative visualization process is detachment. Disconnect yourself from the outcome you intend to see manifest in your life, and observe as the universe creates what it is you desire. Be patient and awake for every opportunity that presents itself. Everyday opportunities come packaged in ways we least expect.

With this mindset, and with the correct physical training, the correct diet and proper rest, you are preparing professionally. This can be the difference between winning and losing, success and failure. You must practise, practise, practise, and set aside some time each day for your creative visualizations, preferably once in the morning when you wake up, and once in the evening before you go to sleep. Once you have mastered these simple steps, you will see your life transforming in miraculous ways.

Positive vision and thoughts powered by your emotions enable you to rediscover your creative power. Winning is the by-product of preparation, so focus on your preparations. What you are thinking and feeling right now you are creating. You can determine your journey and your future.

Therefore set your focus to conquer your fears and weaknesses, and control your emotions by converting stress into vitality.

AGILITY

Producing more competent and fitter dancers is fundamental to the ability to think fast, adapt quickly and to develop a body fit for purpose. Today, the most successful dancers adopt a scientific approach to improving and maintaining fitness levels. Avoiding injury and employing and regularly benefiting from the support of good physiotherapy is fundamental to the enhancement of performance for all dancers and teachers. Correct warm-ups, stretching and cool-downs are crucial in all forms of dance – and particularly to Irish dance because of its physicality. Self-awareness and avoidance of injury are crucial for 'the body beautiful'.

For this section of the SAP programme, I am indebted to Bernadette Flynn for contributions and advice; Bernadette was lead dancer and dance captain in Lord of the Dance for over fifteen years, and now runs, with her husband, the highly successful Flynn-O'Kane Dance School in Co. Tipperary. I am also indebted to James Moran, a highly successful sportsman who played hurling for Limerick, and a fully qualified strength and conditioner instructor at Setanta Sports College. He has recently implemented a functional movement programme for youths aged twelve to eighteen in Limerick.

Functional Movement Programmes

Functional movement in terms of training strengthens and conditions the body to be able to produce strength and power suited to dance. Body conditioning is important to produce competent, fitter dancers whilst at the same time enhancing Irish dance skills and creating awareness of the physical aspects. These programmes are built around the following recognized fitness procedures:

- Warm-up sessions.
- Cool-down sessions.
- Stretching and strengthening.
- Functional movement screening – a proactive approach to reduce the risk of injury.

The programmes take a holistic approach to strengthening and conditioning, and benefit not only the competitive dancer but also those who participate for recreational purposes. They need regular practice.[29,30] The major benefits for all levels are these:

- Better bone density.
- A greater sense of wellbeing.
- More mobility/range of movement around joints.
- Evidence of improved academic scores.

In the long term this will result in a healthier, happier dancer and provide an insight into a scientific approach to fitness fused with dance.

The Functional Competence Model

The purpose of a functional competence model is to assess total body strength and mobility, and is usually carried out by a professional and fully qualified coach. The assessment identifies the functional weaknesses that, when corrected, reduce the risk of injury and improve potential performance. Once the compensation in movement, and the reasons why, have been identified, corrective exercises can be prescribed. If an athlete or dancer does not have functional competence such as stability, mobility and balance, they will not be able to perform the fundamental movement skill – for example, jumping and landing properly – and therefore will not be able to perform effectively the sports-specific skill. Functional competence is the basis that needs to be in place correctly for other attributes to follow.

A competent teacher or coach, no matter what the physical activity, will have a keen interest in teaching and coaching the skills related to that activity. The teacher will usually assume that if a dancer or athlete practises the skills involved they will become better, more efficient and more effective. There tends to be a philosophy of looking for 'winners' in the early and mid-teenage years. The chase for immediate competition skill, speed, strength, power, agility and endurance often dominates the teacher's training plans as they strive to have a winner at all ages. This is a major limitation in many of the strategies employed by teachers, and may result in vital functional development being missed.

The aim of the SAP programme is to give teachers the information to assess and develop the dancer with best practice, with the most up-to-date information available.

Longer-Term Development

The major problem with the competition approach is in the large number of dancers and athletes with limitations in their physical and technical qualities as they mature. Consideration therefore needs to be given to the long-term process of development. The overriding strategy must be to develop the all-round dancer before focusing solely on dance-specific development. It is important to remember that the older the dancer or athlete becomes, the harder it is to right the 'wrongs' of the past. At senior level of elite performance, the occurrence of injury or the failure of a skill under pressure can be traced back to a mismanaged development stage. Dancers will be more equipped to sustain and survive the rigours

Warm-ups with Peter O'Grady.

of training at elite level if they are carefully encouraged through developing and maintaining the base of proper functional movement.

When a sound technical development programme is followed it not only helps to improve performance but also to prevent injury. Taking a holistic approach that is safe for children yields other benefits, including increased strength, enhancement of fitness skills and sports performance, injury prevention, improved psychosocial well-being, better bone density, and better overall health of the child.

The SAP programme gives the teacher the opportunity to screen the dancer for limitations in movement, and then to provide specific individual exercises in their training programme to allow them to become more stable during movement patterns. This then helps improve their performance. When dealing with younger dancers this is an opportune time to commence exercises to tackle such problems. With older dancers this information will also help in the prescription of corrective exercises and the individualization of their training.

It is therefore important to be fully fit in order to improve your agility and avoid injury, and to build your stamina to reach your full potential in dance performance.

PREPARATION

The final section in our SAP programme is all about being fully prepared for all aspects of the project in hand, whether it be performing in the finals of a major dance competition, or taking a TCRG teacher examination, or joining a dance show. This is probably the most important section and crucial for ultimate success. The major areas requiring attention are knowledge, mindset, nutrition and physicality. Some of these, particularly knowledge and mindset, have been discussed elsewhere so only reference will be made to the appropriate chapter, but more detail is now included on nutrition and physicality.

Knowledge

Clearly a detailed knowledge of the subject(s) in hand is fundamental, and it goes without saying that revision of, and familiarization with the topic is essential. More information concerning the following areas can be found as indicated:

- Preparation for exams: Chapter 6.
- Preparations for dance competitions: Chapter 2 and Chapter 6.
- Teaching of solo and céilí dancing: Chapter 4 and Chapter 5.

Mindset

Mindset has been discussed earlier in this chapter, and some of the concepts, steps and recommendations given in this section might be used in this context. It may also be advisable and necessary to seek professional support and further training in some of the ideas proposed.

NUTRITION

Good nutrition has been mentioned on several occasions, but little has actually been said as to what is *meant* by good nutrition. I am indebted to Mary Kerin for her contributions and advice in the preparation of this section.[24] Mary is fully qualified and trained in nutritional and bio-energy therapy, and has qualifications in social sciences, business studies, IT and web design. She currently works as a consultant in the fields of nutrition and natural health solutions. This section will explore the importance and practice of good nutrition – or in our case, fuelling the dancer.

Fuelling Your Dance

You have the capability to supercharge your performance and endurance by controlling what you put on your plate. Vigorous dancing asks a great deal of your body, but thankfully there are many great yet simple ways to upgrade your diet, giving you that extra fuel needed for dancing – especially in the lead-up to and during competitions. 'Nutrition cannot substitute for raw talent, training, mental preparation or equipment, but bad nutrition can destroy performance.'[24]

Fuelling your dance is all about giving your body everything it needs so that it is able to meet your own expectations. If you are asking it, and expect it, to give optimum performance, then you need to help it. Become aware of your food and drink choices. With each choice, ask yourself if you are supporting your body to perform as you would like it to perform – or not! There is always a good, a better and a best choice. You can always, *always* do something to support your energy and your performance – it is all down to the choices that you make.

You need to give your body the right fuel to help sustain its energy and its powers of endurance for the time required, whether that is a few hours or a full day. Give it the ingredients to support its recovery, and to repair what needs repair after all dance sessions, however long or short. It needs to mop up, cool down, and switch down many systems during the hours after intense dance. And it is the food and drink we consume that provides the vitamins, minerals and antioxidants to ensure it recovers, and that we are not setting ourselves up for injuries and issues down the line. All intense activity – whether it is dancing or running, or whatever the sport – is a stress on the body. So every time you are dancing for an hour or two or more, you are depleting your body of vitamins and minerals, and if you don't replace them through the food you eat, then the body naturally starts pulling from tissues and bones to maintain balance – and this can explain cramps and injuries.

This isn't just about fuelling the body for physical performance – our diet also hugely impacts how focused, how calm and sharp we are, the quality of our sleep, hormone production and balance – all of which are cornerstones of health.

At the most basic level you need to ensure that you are not burning up more energy/nutrients than you are fuelling for. You risk draining your body's reserves and damaging your body if you are not providing it with the ingredients – or enough of the right nutrients – to fuel your dance. Don't compromise your health for peak performance.

It's very simple: we will have imbalance in our body if we don't eat the right things, or if we don't eat enough of the right things – and there is strong evidence to suggest that often it is the things that we remove or exclude from our diet that most influence our health, even more so than those that we add in.

The Importance of a Good Diet

Top of the list in the maintenance of a good diet is to *stop eating crap.* Used in abbreviated form CRAP might stand for the following:

C: carbonated or fizzy drinks.
R: refined sugar – and this refers not only to sugar itself, but also to all those products that are made up mostly of sugar, such as sweets, cakes and biscuits.
A: artificial foods/colours/flavouring – in particular the artificial sweetener aspartame and the artificial flavour MSG (monosodium glutamate).
P: processed foods in general.

The problem is that all these foods provide little or no nutrition to the body – some can actually be called anti-nutrients. They are only draining your body of crucial vitamins, minerals and co-factors that are needed for optimum functioning and body balance. Even mild nutrient deficiencies can really influence performance and recovery – which means that if you are slightly lacking in certain minerals or vitamins, you may not have the nutrients in your body that you need to dance to your best ability. For example, every piece of sugar you consume burns up magnesium in your body. Magnesium is one of the *key* minerals necessary for your muscles and every organ in your body to work correctly.

Sugary foods and drinks that give a temporary boost can keep us locked in a cycle of high and low energy. Blood sugars and energy can crash soon after indulging in sugar, or foods that contain sugar, and even foods that quickly convert into sugar (such as breakfast cereals, processed bread, biscuits, bars and sweets). Low blood-sugar levels make us feel hungry, tired, headachy, cranky, lacking in focus.

These issues can be avoided by eating foods that keep blood sugars stable, such as high-quality protein as in eggs, healthy fats such as avocados, and naturally high-quality complex carbohydrates from vegetables, oats and quinoa, for example, and not carbohydrates from junk foods, such as white breads and processed foods.

It you were to take one action to improve your performance and recovery, let that be to cut down on all those things that are high in sugar. On competition days if you consume a lot of sugary junk then your body will be busy trying to stabilize blood sugars and you will find that it will have diverted the energy you need for that perfect performance – your body is always trying to keep balance and protect you from crises – and high and low sugar are a crisis to the body!

If your breakfast is a bowl of cereal then you have maxed out on your sugar quota for the day before you even get up from the breakfast table. Look at the most popular breakfast cereals – in most cases nearly half of each spoonful is sugar, besides which it is a processed food so it converts to sugar again in the body – so it is basically sugar for breakfast.

Eat Good Quality Carbohydrates, Fats and Proteins
In all that you eat and drink, opt for the versions that will support your body, and not challenge it – therefore opt for the best, most nutritious version, opt for good quality protein, fats, carbohydrates.

Eat a diet of nutrient-dense colourful and quality foods: this is the foundation of supporting your body and brain, your life and your dance. In order to get the macro- and micronutrients needed it is vital to eat whole real foods. 'Real' food is one ingredient – it does not contain a plethora of added sugars, preservatives, flavourings and a whole host of chemicals – it is not processed food. Foods out of a box or a packet that have five to ten ingredients or more are not real food and lack nutrients and goodness.

When you go to bed at night and recall the meals and snacks taken during the day, if it has been a day of white or beigey-brown foods then it's very likely that you have not taken in a fraction of the nutrients needed to fuel your body's basic requirements, let alone to dance. Your day's foods should include the colours of the rainbow – so let this be your effort, starting today.

It all goes back to the simple rule of eating fresh, whole, real foods with plenty of colour and variety. Carbohydrates in the form of complex carbohydrates are centre stage: vegetables and fruit, with a focus on berries, wholegrains, oats, beans. Make particular effort to include green vegetables every day as they provide you with minerals (such as magnesium) and vitamins (the B vitamins, including folate) that are crucial to normal body function, and in particular when you are asking body and mind for intense activity.

Sufficient or optimal protein intake is vital. Protein is needed to repair and build muscles, and it provides the building blocks for so many systems in the body, such as the hormonal system and the immune system. We need it to produce enzymes that help us break down our foods, and to switch certain body functions on and off. There are varying levels of protein in all whole foods. Again, it is all about focusing on nutrient-dense sources of protein such as eggs, quality fish, poultry, meat, nuts, seeds, quinoa, chia seeds. You need to take in some protein with every meal and snack – and this is an important rule for every day, and not just for dance days. So if you are having some fruit, be sure to have, for example, some nuts or seeds or nut butter with it.

Fats are crucial for physical and mental health. 'Good' fats, which include omega 3 fats, are obtained from cold-water fish such as mackerel and salmon, from nuts and seeds, grass-fed meat and green vegetables. A whole-food diet also helps to ensure that you consume plenty of antioxidants, which help with physical repair in the event of muscle damage and injury, and aid recovery after strenuous physical effort.

Antioxidants are present in colourful fruit and vegetables; good sources include fruit and vegetables that are dark in colour (especially orange, red, purple) and for example green tea and cherry concentrate.

Hydration and Electrolyte Balance is Key

The two main nutritional causes for sore and cramping muscles are poor hydration – which equates to not taking in enough fluids – and electrolyte imbalance. Therefore one of the single most vital aspects of fuelling your dance is optimal hydration. Water is one of the most important nutrients in your dance diet, and you need to drink it before, during and after dance.

Your dance performance is massively influenced by hydration status. Dehydration leads to an increase in lactic acid, acidity in the body, muscle cramps and tiredness, while proper hydration and restorative fluids help to maintain normal muscle function, and to reduce muscle cramps and tiredness so that you can dance for longer at a stretch. Proper hydration is also necessary to maintain blood volume and regulate body temperature.

What is true hydration? Most people think of hydration as drinking water, but it is actually the process of absorbing water – and electrolytes are instrumental in powering your cells to absorb water. While there is no universal agreement on what defines optimum hydration, there is widespread consensus that it is better to drink water than to drink nothing, and drinks containing electrolytes help promote better performance than water alone.

Electrolytes are mineral salts that are dissolved in and around the cells in our body. They are in our blood, tissues, urine and other body fluids. These salts carry charges and help balance the amount of water in our body, they move nutrients in and waste out of our cells, and therefore play a central role in body processes that are essential for living; for example, they allow heart and muscle fibres to contract and function properly, and they help regulate acidity (pH), body temperature and the generation of energy.

Electrolytes are lost naturally in sweat, so if you are dancing for sixty minutes or more, they need to be replaced into your body so your muscles can still move efficiently, avoiding cramps and fatigue and the risk of dehydration. Sodium, magnesium, calcium, potassium, chlorine, phosphate are all electrolytes, and they are obtained from the foods we eat and the fluids we drink. Fortunately we can maintain electrolyte (and salt) levels naturally by consuming a well-balanced diet.

Electrolytes are a very easy and quick way to replenish, hydrate and restore healthy energy levels, helping you to perform at your best, especially during extended or strenuous dance sessions.

The quantity of electrolytes needed is different for everyone. Some people sweat more or cramp more, and it also depends on the length of the session, the temperature and/or the humidity of the environment – though it is important to remember that you still sweat and lose electrolytes during low-intensity dance and in a cold environment, so never underestimate their importance.

Optimum hydration is therefore unique to you and the factors surrounding your activity, so you should consider the following:

- Your hydration status before beginning a dance routine.
- The need for fluid, electrolyte and substrate replacement during dance.
- The need for restoring water and electrolyte balance afterwards.

Another reason to ensure proper hydration combined with electrolytes is to reduce the occurrence of exercise-induced asthma. How does this happen? A lot of symptoms such as asthma, eczema, red-face, sinus, hives, indicate high levels of histamine. If you become dehydrated, the histamine in the body becomes more concentrated. Alternatively, the more water you drink and absorb, the more that histamine concentration will go down, and fewer histamine-related symptoms will occur.

Optimizing Hydration and Electrolyte Status
Water and electrolytes can be supplied and replenished through the foods we eat as well as the drinks we consume. Plan, pre-prepare and line up your fluids and snacks in advance of intense dance days and classes – at the very least ensure you have upgraded liquids that are easy to reach and readily available. For example, if you are dancing for one hour or less, make sure that you have a supply of good quality water, and maybe a sprinkle

of Himalayan salt (plus chia seeds). For extended sessions of more than one hour, ensure that you have supplies of the following:

- Coconut water, which contains magnesium and potassium. With its natural sugar (simple carbs), minerals (electrolytes) and water, it is the ultimate 'natural gatorade'.
- Water with cherry concentrate, proven to speed recovery and reduce soreness.
- 'Upgraded' water – for example, add Himalayan rock salt/cherry concentrate/chia seeds to the water.
- Green tea – it is high in antioxidants, so add it to smoothies/juices.
- Homemade energy/sports drinks – for example spring water + Himalayan salt + maple syrup + fresh lemon juice.
- A shot of beetroot juice that can be taken before or after the session.

Foods that are particularly hydrating and which provide electrolytes and vitamins include celery, watermelon, bell peppers, cucumbers, strawberries and cantaloupe. Bananas are shown to be more beneficial than an energy drink, as they provide dense and readily available carbohydrates for energy. Add them to smoothies with, for example, coconut water or milk/milled chia or flaxseed/berries. Also useful are the following:

- Water supplemented with high-grade electrolytes, available as powder, liquid or capsules.
- Smoothies (home-made) with banana/avocado/berries/coconut water; shop-bought smoothies can be upgraded with, for example, milled chia/flaxseed.
- Beetroot juice/shots, which boost nitric oxide for improved performance and recovery.

The Benefits of Magnesium

Magnesium is king when it comes to recovery and preventing injury. Magnesium-rich foods include greens, nuts and seeds. The following might also be useful:

- Supplements: aim for quality powders or concentrated magnesium drops – these can be added to drinks and smoothies.
- Transdermal magnesium: this can be sprayed directly on muscles before and after dance with effective results (however, note that with tan and make-up it cannot be used on exposed areas on a competition day).
- Epsom salts are magnesium sulphate: one to two cupfuls can be of benefit in a bath, or when soaking the feet in a basin of water.

The Knock-On Benefits of a Good Diet

Making an effort with your diet will have knock-on benefits for all the systems in your body, and your overall health in general, because every part of our body affects every other part. The associated benefits of a good diet might include the following:

- How well we sleep: never short-change sleep. Our body restores and heals when we sleep – it is when the brain detoxifies, so we need deep sleep, and enough sleep.
- How we relax: the ability to 'switch off' and relax is just as important, if not more important than pushing ourselves to perform.
- How we move in general: this includes time for mindful movement, for tuning in to our body, and learning to listen to our body.

We all have the 'X' factor – and this is not about dance, talent or winning: it is the fact that we all have the capability to help our body reach its full potential, in all that we do and all that we are. We can influence how healthy we are, how energetic we feel, how relaxed and focused we are, by the choices we make every day. The key to unlocking our own X factor lies in our everyday efforts – and these efforts, along with dedication and a natural love for dance, will culminate in the results we dream of.

In Summary

Recommended high quality foods are listed in the following table.

RECOMMENDED HIGH QUALITY FOODS

BREAKFAST	SALADS	SMOOTHIES
Egg-based:	Mixed leaves	Avocado
scrambled	Tomatoes/cherry tomatoes	Banana
boiled	Chopped artichoke (jars)	Berries
omelette	Cooked quinoa or rice	Dates – pitted
poached	Avocado	Hemp
fried in coconut oil	Olives	Kale
	Celery	Nut butter
Chia pudding	Lentils	Cacoa
	Wholegrain rice	Tahini
Oat or millet porridge	Lemon/lime juice	Cinnamon
+ berries and milled chia/flaxseed	Apple (grated)	Choice of milk, preferably
	Spring/red onion	non-dairy
Avocado	Chickpeas	Spinach
	Pasta	Chia
Beans	Olive oil	Flaxseed
	Cucumber	Cherry concentrate
Overnight oats	Beans	Yogurt
	Berries, especially blueberries	Coconut water
Home-made smoothies	Raw grated carrot	Ice
	Boiled egg	Vanilla extract
Pancakes made with oats	Milled flaxseed mix	Milk keflr
+ milled chia/flaxseed, berries	Beetroot	Nuts – e.g. cashew
	Cheese of choice	Ginger
Yoghurt	Toasted seeds	Water
+ fruit/berries	Balsamic vinegar	Quality protein powder
+ crushed nuts/seeds	Crushed nuts of choice	
+ milled chia/flaxseed	Crushed garlic	
	Peppers	
Home-made or quality granola mix	Chopped grapes	
	Fresh herbs/pesto	
If cereal, choose low sugar	Courgette	
+ milled chia/flaxseed mixes	Chicken	
+ berries	Chopped orange	
+ non-dairy milk	Chilli flakes	
	Cooked broccoli	
	Sprouts	
	Plus added cheese/chicken/salmon/	
	sardines or meat of choice	

Recommended snacks are listed in the table below:

Snack Ideas
Fresh berries/fruit + raw, unsalted nuts + seeds.
Fruit with nut butter – spread some nut butter on apple slices, or drizzle on berries/sliced banana.
Roast nuts and seeds in the oven with some tamari sauce.
Mix of nuts of choice and popcorn with pieces of dark chocolate.
Dips (humus, guacamole) with oatcakes/rice cakes/raw vegetable sticks.
Toasted nuts with added maple syrup and Himalayan/sea salt.
Dark chocolate and a handful of nuts.
Yogurt with toppings such as berries/nuts/seeds/milled chia.
Wholegrain, oat or gluten-free crackers with, for example, avocado, tomato, goat's cheese, humus, nut butter, banana.
Smoothies with banana/avocado/berries/coconut water. If shop bought add milled chia/flaxseed++.
Home-made energy bars/balls/muffins.
For sandwiches – top wholegrain or speciality nutrient-dense bread with quality protein of choice such as chicken, turkey, beef, fish, egg with mixed salad.
Tub or cold platter of meat/fish/with salads of choice – mixed, quinoa, lentil, etc.
Choose from the ever-increasing selection of quality snack bars such as Naked, Dr Coys, Pulsin.

Don't Dance on Empty!
On days of extended/intensive dance, such as competition days, the following foods and drinks are recommended:
Pre-dance: Two to four hours before – a large wholefood meal of high-quality nutrients; or one to two hours before – a snack such as a smoothie/oat cracker/wholegrain bread topped with nut butter, milled flaxseed mix, banana or humus. Pre-dance boost – beetroot juice. **During dance:** Hydrate water is sufficient when dancing for less than 60min; for more than 60min upgrade your fluids as detailed above. **Post dance:** Ideally eat within 30–40min. The quality of your recovery is dependent on food choices – these should be nutrient dense and easy to digest. It is also best to eat a wholefood meal within four hours of the dance activity.

The rainbow of colours – this makes for a healthy diet.

PHYSICALITY

The final part of this section on the preparation element of SAP is physicality, and thanks are due to Peter O'Grady for his contribution to this section.[31] Peter is a fully qualified health fitness and sports injury therapist. He specializes in Irish dancer training, and is based in County Mayo, Ireland.

This is all about having a body fit for purpose, in our case dancing, and it will cover two areas, namely exercising and physiotherapy. Topics discussed in this chapter include:

- Understanding how the human body adapts to stress (exercise).
- Knowing how to prepare your body before placing large amounts of stress upon it.
- Exercise specificity for Irish dancing.

General Adaptation Syndrome

The human body will adapt to the stress that is placed upon it. This includes both physical and mental stress. The process of adaptation due to stress is known as 'general adaptation syndrome' (GAS). Understanding how our body reacts to training helps us to know how we should train dancers – or anyone for that matter. When you see a bodybuilder making massive gains or a person lose lots of weight over time, this is GAS in practice.

Dr Hans Selye was the medical researcher credited with the discovery of GAS. He was the first professional to give a technical term to the observation of how organisms change when exposed to a stimulus. It was he who also said that an organism's

stress response can be broken down into three stages.

The body first reacts to stress by entering the alarm stage ('fight or flight'), when the body prepares for physical activity. Your body's immediate response during this phase is stiffness and soreness, and as a result, there may be a reduction in performance. The fitter you get, the greater the stress and stimuli needed to induce shock. How your body reacts will determine which stage you visit next.

Next is the resistance stage, where the body tries to adapt in order to cope with the stress by trying to bring the body back to normal following an initial stressor. Unlike stage one, your body will be able to tolerate the stress a bit better. Biological reactions occur when resting including hormonal adaptations, nervous system adaptations and muscle tissue building, to name a few, making you a better version of yourself the next day. These adaptations will differ for each person, and some people will bounce back better than others.

Lastly, if your body has endured high levels of stress for a long period of time, you will likely start to feel physical effects such as fatigue and a decrease in energy. This occurs when the stimulus and stress used in training were too much for the body to handle. Maybe the athlete was asked to do too many sprints or maybe the dancer was asked to do too many steps with little recovery time. This is known as the exhaustion stage, and it is a stage that should be avoided at all costs.

The Irish dance trainer and dance teacher role is to assess what type of stress (exercise) is needed to optimize the dancing athlete's performance.

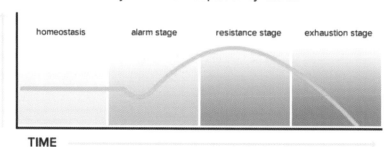

Graphical representation of the Hans Selye general adaptation syndrome.

They design the appropriate exercise programme or dance class, and instruct the proper execution of the programme. Too much of any type of stress can have a negative effect on an athlete's health and performance, so try to avoid exercises that target the same movements or muscles. Identifying good stressors (eustress) may decrease bad stressors (distress) and improve an athlete's overall health and performance.

When stress (exercise) causes the body to increase effort more than usual, the body has been put into a situation of overload. Overload will temporarily decrease the athlete's ability to do work and to do work efficiently (work capacity). When the body recovers from the original bout of exercise, its work capacity increases. Not only is the correct amount of exercise or stress important, but so is *recovery*. When the stress being put on the body is too intense and recovery time is insufficient, this results in *overtraining*. Then you have the opposite to that: if the amount of recovery time given to the athlete is too much, this results in *detraining*.

Good quality and quantity of training, together with good quality and quantity of recovery, leads to faster and better results!

In the preparation of Irish dancers for major competitions or show performances, overtraining is quite common. When this happens, the dancer's performance will worsen, and not get better. It is the Irish dance trainer and dance teacher's job to work together to find the right balance of exercise stress and recovery in all aspects of the dancer's training.

All great programmes have one thing in common: progressive overload. This is the gradual increase in weight, volume, intensity, frequency or time training to achieve a specific goal. The small incremental improvements that you make each time you attempt a strength exercise or lace up your dancing shoes and see improvements, is progressive overload in action. If you are not attempting to improve or progress in some way, it's probably not training. This is why a thorough understanding of progressive overload and GAS is an absolute necessity.

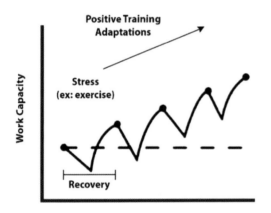

The relationship between work capacity and time for optimum training.

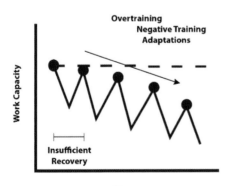

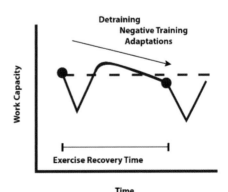

More relationships between work capacity and time, illustrating overtraining and detraining.

In summary, the perfect adaptation is when you train to maximize the time spent in the resistance stage while avoiding any time spent in the exhaustion stage.

Movement Preparation

The first phase of any training session, dance practice session or competition performance is the 'warm-up phase', as you would know it best. Studies have shown that a warm-up specifically emphasizes the role of heating the body, including the muscles prior to training, as well as benefiting us in many other areas including improved joint mobility, improved elasticity in the muscles for more strenuous activity, and an increase in injury prevention. All this information is quite correct, however, the general conception of 'warm-up' does not adequately capture what needs to happen prior to training and competitions, and trainers now use 'movement preparation' as an alternative to the term 'warm-up'.

As a dancer, you are preparing your body to move specifically for Irish dancing, which will include many different movements from different parts of the body. Use this movement preparation phase as an integrated approach to prepare you physically and mentally for the demands of training and competition through a progressive and specific preparation period.

Creating a Better Movement Preparation Routine
The goals are almost always the same when designing a movement preparation routine:

- To follow the most recent strength and conditioning principles while making the movement preparation routine more Irish dancing specific.
- To minimize injuries and to prepare for maximal performance at each practice.

There may be a lot of variation in the exact exercises included in your dancing athlete's movement preparation routine, but do try to include all the following components:

- Soft tissue preparation.
- General movement preparation/non-impact based joint and muscular preparation.

- Metabolic/cardiovascular preparation, including specific movement patterns (focus on the planes of motion).
- Advanced Irish dancing specific dynamic stretching.
- Core activation and control (focusing on the correct breathing pattern).
- Irish dancing specific core activation and control.
- Jumping and landing mechanics.
- Fundamental Irish dancing skills and drills.

Exercise Specificity for Irish Dancing

Irish dance trainers understand that training for Irish dancing is a very specific type of need. By definition, specificity seeks to target the various factors needed to facilitate training adaptations that will respond to a stimulus (exercise or programme). With all modes of training or exercises included in your programme design, specificity is determined by considering all the following factors:

- The required muscle actions involved.
- The speed of the movements used.
- The range of motion.
- Metabolic demands.
- Training intensity and volume.

Many coaches only think of specificity in terms of resistance training; however, since there are other very specific needs for an Irish dancing athlete, the need for specificity also applies to other modes of training, and your programme should reflect those needs.

When making decisions for programme design, one needs to keep in mind the general principles of strength training and conditioning. First, consider which muscle groups need to be targeted for Irish dancing and the timeline of the training planning. The most likely forms of methods used follow the principles of undulating periodization. This means that increased demands are imposed on the dancers in the name of progression. Undulating periodization involves the relationship between a stimulus presented to the body, and the recovery from the stimulus over time.

Some of the variables that are incorporated into programme designs are strength, endurance, power and cardiovascular types of training. The goal is to train the dancer's strengths while improving weaknesses. This may be done on completely different levels. For example, the dancer might still have needs in the lower stages of the pyramid for improvement, but typically the programme design for your Irish dancing athlete is in the higher stages as your most relevant framework. Therefore, you will be managing a lot of different types of training for each level.

One major objective of the strength training programme for Irish dancers is to improve the overall structural integrity of the musculoskeletal system, and all major muscle groups should be given equal emphasis. Structural exercises are considered to be those that require loading through the vertebral column, and should be considered for their value in helping the Irish dancer avoid injury. A great example would be a single leg squat. This type of multi-joint exercise will have an excellent transfer to Irish dancing.

Typically, there will be weeks of notice before a scheduled event because Irish dancing organizations will have their events planned up to a year in advance. The dancing athlete and the dance teacher would have decided on the dancer's schedule well in advance. With this in mind, it is probably best to understand that the Irish dancer will most likely require high levels of aerobic and anaerobic conditioning throughout the entire year.

Even though there is no substitute for training for Irish dancing except dancing, there are ways to design a metabolic conditioning programme that will create the metabolic demands of the athlete's Irish dancing performance. Using well designed metabolic conditioning programmes makes sense for Irish dancing training, as the risk for injury to the Irish dancing athlete would be far greater if the training protocol were limited to continual high-intensity dancing sessions.

Since we see that metabolic conditioning programmes such as circuit training (including circuit weight training) fit the training needs of the Irish dancing athlete, teachers are encouraged to use the information known about the dancer's performance demands by developing programme designs that are in accordance with the established number of dances at a competition as well as the length of the dances in any upcoming events or competitions.

With specificity in mind, metabolic conditioning for Irish dancing would consist of movements and exercises that are specific for Irish dancing. Have the dancers perform a training routine that reflects a 2.5min dancing performance, followed by rest to allow the dancer to recover enough so that they can continue to train at an intensity that reflects their performance. If the dancer is a show dancer, then they might have to complete a training routine that takes longer, depending on their performance demands.

In summary, regular and structured exercising has many benefits. Most forms of dance require different types of physical abilities – and some, such as Irish dancing, require strength, endurance, balance, flexibility and grace. There is a wide range of different exercises available, but for the Irish dancer these can be split into three main types: general exercises, strength exercises and specific exercises for Irish dancers.

General Exercises

The following exercises are useful on a general level:

Cardiovascular: Such as running and jogging, which promote stamina and strength and will help your cardio performance – they will also help you feel lighter, and will help with the ease of dance.

Stretches: Are invaluable, and it is recommended that you stretch every day for thirty minutes, with each stretch taking around ninety seconds. Stretching helps the muscle groups expand, improving all-round flexibility, and helps you twist more easily.

Push-ups: Help strengthen the chest, arms and back, and are very useful in improving posture and helping your balance.

Correct exercises reduce the risk of injury and the need for physiotherapy – for example aerobic exercise...

... or a hamstring stretch...

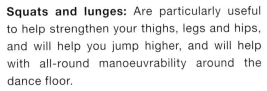

... or bar drills...

... and a proper cool-down.

Squats and lunges: Are particularly useful to help strengthen your thighs, legs and hips, and will help you jump higher, and will help with all-round manoeuvrability around the dance floor.

Sit-ups: Help your hips and arms and the whole body.

Strength Exercises

Amongst other things, dancing requires strength, and muscular and cardiovascular endurance. It is crucial that dancers protect their joints and muscles, and strength is the main weapon against injury. Recommended routines involve doing circuit training three times a day, two to three times a week.

The moves include aids such as resistance bands, kettlebells and medicine balls.

Specific Exercises for Irish Dancers
These exercises feature interesting variations on the basic exercising steps referred to above, together with details of ab exercises, hamstring stretches, warm-up routines and planks. Routines are directed towards improving areas such as the hips, posture, legs, arms, ankles, knee and foot strength, back flexibility and leg straightening, and improving rocks, improving jumps and losing weight.

PHYSIOTHERAPY

It is vitally important that all Irish dancers take very good care of their health and body, and when injured that they take expert advice and treatment from professionally qualified physiotherapists or trainers without delay. There are a number of excellent practitioners who specialize in Irish dancing, such as Peter O'Grady, who has assisted with the previous paragraphs. He has published an excellent book entitled *Upping your Step*, and has prepared a number of videos that are available on-line.[31] These feature details and advice on factors such as injury and recovery, the foundations of effective training, scaling your health and performance warm-ups and cool-downs, strength training for Irish dancers, balance training, flexibility, conditioning for Irish dancers and training plans.

The majority of dance-related injuries are caused by overuse and/or misuse, as opposed to any sort of trauma. The foot, ankle, lower leg, back and hips are some of the most common injury areas, although many other dancing injuries can occur. Most of these are easily prevented, with focus on specific dance techniques, flexibility and strength, and the exercises highlighted in the previous section.

The following are symptoms of some typical Irish dancing injuries:

Plantar fasciitis: A painful injury that occurs when the tissue supporting the arch of the foot is overused and becomes inflamed.

Bunions: Small deformations of the bone around the big toe area, often caused by wearing ill-fitting dance shoes.
Shin splints: A very painful condition caused by slight tears of the tissue that connect the muscle to the tibia/shin bone, caused by over-exertion of the lower limbs by landing after a jump on a hard surface, or by landing incorrectly.
Achilles tendinopathy: A condition in which the Achilles tendon has become irritated and degenerative.

The types of injury commonly experienced by Irish dancers are very similar to other dance genres such as ballet, where problems with big toe tendons, outer shin tendons and hip muscles are common. Treatments frequently used today include stretching and strengthening drills to ensure that the core, hip, knee and ankle joints all work in unison to keep the foot in an optimal position. Orthotics can be used to help support the foot, particularly during non-dancing periods when it is out of the dancing shoe, thus enabling adequate resting of the surrounding joints and muscles. Sports massage is also found to be beneficial in helping to heal over-used muscles.

HEALTH AND SAFETY MANAGEMENT IN DANCE SCHOOLS

For those involved in teaching, managing a dance school or contemplating opening a dance school, several additional health and safety factors are of significant importance. These relate to health and safety legislation, and good practice in working with children and adolescents. As with all other businesses an Irish dance school, its employees, volunteers and pupils have a responsibility to ensure their safety and welfare. In particular, I wish to highlight four major areas:

- The essentials for working with children.
- Paediatric first aid.
- Emergency planning.
- Risk analysis.

Working with Children in a Safe Environment

Child protection is absolutely fundamental and mandatory in all forms of education and activities involving children and young adults. This has now become universal and is an essential part of the ethos, management and accountability of any registered Irish dance school. All the major regulatory organizations have stringent procedures in place to protect children. In 2002 CLRG implemented its comprehensive Child Protection Policy, and in 2009 published its Vetting Policy as a further step in the extension of the Child Protection Policy. This has since been updated (February 2020), and this latest version can be found on their website.[8] The full protection policy is forty-eight pages long, and it is inappropriate to repeat all this in detail in this guide, but it is recommended that the reader refers to the CLRG website for the full text.

Child Protection Policy
The CLRG policy states the following:

> It recognises that the safety and welfare of children and young people is of paramount importance, and is committed to taking appropriate steps to ensure the safety and well-being of the children and young people with whom they engage, regardless of class, gender, race, creed, age or ability. CLRG has a 'zero tolerance' policy with regard to abuse, intimidation, bullying (physical or emotional), racism and sexist behaviour directed towards children and young people. They acknowledge the right of children and young people to be treated with respect at all times, to be listened to and to have their views taken into consideration in matters that affect them.

Vetting Procedures
The Child Protection Policy of CLRG requires that all persons be vetted or have background checks carried out, to ensure that they are suitable and proper persons to have access to children or vulnerable persons, in order to teach Irish dancing, as well as carrying out work or activities relating to teaching, or related activities involving Irish dancing. The following requirements are compulsory for all teachers:

- They must be vetted by an approved body in their country of origin – for example The Garda in Ireland.
- They must attend child protection training.
- They must uphold CLRG's Child Protection and Welfare Policy and Code of Practice.

Paediatric First Aid

Most Irish dance schools have classes for pupils up to twenty-one years of age and above, but a large number are within the age range four to eighteen years and are particularly vulnerable to sickness and injury. It is recommended that school owners, teachers and volunteers have some knowledge of paediatric first aid.

Attendance at a recognized paediatric first-aid training course is encouraged. Suitable courses are available on-line or at training centres with organizations such as The British Red Cross and St John Ambulance.[32,33] These courses cover the essential elements to provide effective first aid at dance classes and within the dance school and feis venues. Courses typically cover the areas described below.

Primary Level
Candidates should know the following:

- The contents of a first-aid box.
- What to do if the patient is unresponsive both when breathing and when not breathing.
- How to check airways.
- How to conduct a primary survey on a child.

Secondary Level
Candidates should know the following:

- When to call an ambulance.
- How to put children and infants into the recovery position.
- How to deal with unconscious casualties.

- How to respond to choking, wounds and bleeding.
- How to treat shock.

Secondary Injuries

Candidates should be able to deal with/treat secondary injuries, such as:

- Burns and scalds.
- Eye injuries.
- Head injuries.
- Fractures and broken bones.
- Spinal injuries.
- Sickness and fever.

Resuscitation, CPR for Children and Infants

Candidates should know the following:

- How to administer CPR to infants and children.
- When to stop CPR.
- How to use a defibrillator.

Secondary Illnesses and Conditions

Candidates should know how to deal with the following:

- Asthma.
- Allergic reactions and anaphylaxis.
- Bites and stings.
- Diabetes.
- Epilepsy.
- High temperatures.
- Hyperventilation.
- Electric shock.

Additional Secondary Illnesses and Conditions

Candidates should understand the importance of recognizing the following:

- Sickle cell.
- Meningitis and septicaemia.
- Sepsis.
- Croup.
- Nose bleeds.
- Sprains and strains.
- Poisoning.

- Smoke inhalation.
- Hypothermia and drowning.

Successful completion of these types of course is rewarded with a Paediatric First Aid Certificate that meets the requirements specified by OFSTED and can be used as evidence for an NVQ in childcare.

Emergency Planning

For businesses, including dance schools, emergency preparedness planning can make the difference between staying in business and losing everything. Having an emergency plan, however simple, is one of the easiest ways to help ensure your dance school survives and recovers from an emergency. Protecting the safety and lives of individuals, particularly children, is the first priority during an emergency situation. Emergency evacuation planning will help reduce confusion, minimize injuries and ultimately save lives. A large number of organizations, including the HSE, can advise on the content and procedures required, and these can be found on the internet.

Risk Analysis

What is a Risk Assessment?

The UK-based Health and Safety Executive (HSE) says: 'A risk assessment is nothing more than a careful examination of what, in work and the workplace, could cause harm to people.' In the UK, employers have a duty under the Management of Health and Safety at Work Regulations 1999 to carry out risk assessments to identify what hazards exist in a workplace, and how likely these hazards are to cause harm. They must then decide what prevention or control measures are needed.

Details and recommendations focusing on the following areas can be readily found in HSE publications:

- How should employers carry out a risk assessment?
- Who should carry out the risk assessment?
- The five steps for a risk assessment.
- How an employer should deal with hazards.
- How often risk assessments should take place.

In summary, the Management of Health and Safety at Work Regulations 1999 set out safety management guidance for employers for tackling risks. The basic approach is also known as a 'hierarchy of control', because it sets out the order in which employers must approach risk management.[34]

The wheel of success.

CONCLUDING REMARKS

In a society that worships love, freedom and beauty, dance is sacred. It is a remembrance of the past, a joyful exclamation of thanks for the good of the present and a prayer for the future.

Amelia Atwater-Rhodes

Hopefully this guide will provide its readers with a comprehensive and complete insight into the world and practice of Irish dancing. It is more than just an instruction manual on how to dance an Irish jig: it also embraces many aspects of Irish history, culture and ethics, and highlights other individual benefits in physical and mental health. Dancers also benefit from improved self-confidence, and the learning process helps to instil a discipline that is advantageous in other aspects of modern life.

The control of regulated dance schools offers parents the reassurance that their child will be fully protected by the child protection processes and the house rules that are in place. Irish dance schools are very family oriented, and are not only a teaching forum, but also centres and a focus for social gatherings. This social element, in a safe environment, offers youngsters the benefits of learning about and participating in Irish culture, and other cultures as the global nature of Irish dancing expands.

Irish dancing offers a young newcomer the opportunity of an enjoyable hobby as well as realistic and rewarding career opportunities in a range of closely work-related activities. It is a wonderful experience to be able to follow a career in an area that is also one's passion and love.

The world of Irish dancing was very badly impacted by the covid pandemic that hit the world at the start of 2020. Dance classes, feiseanna and shows all stopped as the world battled to control the spread of the virus. Many dancing activities were put on hold for around eighteen months, although Zoom classes were introduced for the committed enthusiasts, enabling them to maintain their interest. Fortunately, at the time of writing (October 2021) the world is beginning to recover, and Irish dancing is at the forefront of this.

There is no doubt that Irish dancing has a great future ahead. Dance classes have restarted, the shows are restarting, and competitions are being held world-wide, with the prestigious 50th World Championships being held in Belfast in April 2022. One of the benefits arising from the pandemic has been the increasing use of social media outlets in the field of Irish dancing. This has seen, and will continue to see, more and more innovators exploring creative choreography through these channels.

This guide can surely be part of this rebirth, and it offers newcomers a roadmap to an exciting future in Irish dancing.

Irish fancy dress!

Lord of the Dance.

Lord of the Dance in front of the lights.

Ella Owens in flight.

Céim Óir dancers at play.

Dancers in Amersham on St Patrick's Day.

Marie with Michael Flatley and Ronan Hardiman.

SUPPLIERS OF IRISH DANCE WEAR

COSTUMES

Eire Designs by Gavin Doherty: www.gavindoherty.co.uk
John Carey Design: info@johncareydesign.ie
Doire Dress Designs: www.doiredressesdesign.com
Taylor Irish Dance Dresses: taylordresses@hotmail.co.uk
Elevation Design Ireland: www.elevationdesign.ie
Elite Dance Designs: www.elitedancedesigns.com
Eileen Plater Irish Dance Dresses: www.eileenplater.com
Conor O'Sullivan designs: www.instagram.com › conorosullivandesign.com

FOOTWEAR

Antonio Pacelli Ltd: www.antoniopacelli.com
Oriel Irish Dance Supplies: www.orielirishdancesupplies.com
Hallmore Dance Products: www.hallmoredanceproducts.ie
Rutherford Irish Shoes: www.rutherfordshoes.com
Dancia International: www.dancia.co.uk
Feis Fayre: www.feisfayre.com
Feis Wear: www.feiswear.com
The Irish Dance Shop: www.irishdanceshop.com
The Irish Dancer: www.theirishdancer.co.uk
Georgielocks: www.georgielocksdanceshop.com
iDance Irish: www.idanceirish.co.uk
Fays Shoes: www.fays-shoes.com

HEADWEAR

Paula's Wigs and Blings: www.paulaswigsandbling.com
Camelia Rose: www.cameliarosewigs.co.uk
World of Irish Dancing: Melanie Murphy: www.worldofirishdancing.com

THE LANGUAGE OF IRISH DANCE

THE LANGUAGE (TERMINOLOGY) OF IRISH DANCE

English word	Gaelic	Definition
Bar		A unit into which a musical piece can be divided for Irish dance commonly uses an eight-bar step
Body		The section of a ceílí dance that is repeated a number of times
Reel	Cór/ril	
Hornpipe	Cornphiopa	
Jig	Port	
Dance	Rince	
Solo dance	Rince aonair	
Solo set dance	Rince leithleach	
Set dance		A solo hard-shoe dance choreographed to a particular tune in which the skill and competency of the dancer is showcased
Step		The transfer of weight from one foot to the ball or heel of the other foot
Step dancing		The name for Irish dance from the time of the dance masters
Tempo		Speed or pace of the underlying musical beat
Traditional set dance		Composed by the eighteenth-century dance masters showcasing footwork e.g. St Patrick's Day
	Árd-ghád	Dancers competing at open level
	Ár Rincí Fóirne	A collection of ceílí dances published by CLRG
Boy	Buachaillí	
	Bun-ghrád	Dancers competing at beginners' level
Girl	Cailiní	
Musician	Ceoltóir	
Programme	Clár	

Continued

English word	Gaelic	Definition
	Coiste Faire	Committee overseeing regulations at feiseanna
Competition	Comórtas	
Men	Fir	
Soft shoes	Ghillies	
	Méan-ghrád	Dancers performing at intermediate level
Adjudicator	Moltóir	
Teacher	Múinteoir	
	Oireachtas	A major step dance competition
	Rialacha	Rules or regulations for a competition
Figure dance	Rinci fóirne	
Irish dance school	Scoil rinci	
Senior	Sinsir	
Junior	Sóisir	
TCRG	TCRG	Title that indicates a teacher is registered with An Coimisiun or Comhdháil to teach solo and ceílí dances
TMRF	TMRF	Title that indicates a teacher is registered with An Coimisiun or Comhdháil to teach ceílí dances only
	Tús-ghrád	Dancers competing at primary level
Step	Céim	
Clog dance		Nineteenth-century term that covered all forms of percussive dance
Cotillion		Popular ballroom dance performed in the eighteenth century – the basis of many modern-day ceílí dances
Dance	Damhsa	
Quadrille		Ballroom dance popular in France and adapted by dance masters

BIBLIOGRAPHY

Cullinane, Dr J, *Irish Dancing Commission – Its Origins and Evolution*.
Ni Bhriain, O, *The Terminology of Irish Dance* (Macater Press 2008).
Ni Bhriain, O, and McCabe, M, *Jigs to Jacobites* (Independent Publishing Network, Dublin 2018).

REFERENCES

1   Claddagh Design: website article 'A Brief History and Guide' www.claddaghdesign.com
2   Irelands Eye: website article 'Irish Dance' www.irelandseye.com/irishdance
3   BBC: website article 'A Short History of Irish Dance' www.bbc.co.uk/irisharticles
4   'Ask About Ireland' dance music: www.askaboutireland.ie/dancemusicinstruments
5   Ireland's Eye: article 'Irish dance – the music': www.irelandseye.com/irishdancemusic
6   Dr John Cullinane: *Irish Dancing Commission – Its Origins and Evolution*.
7   'Self-Directed Learning', University of Waterloo, Centre for Teaching Excellence: website: uwaterloo.ca
8   *An Coimisiún le Rincí Gaelacha* (CLRG): website: www.clrg.ie
9   *An Comhdháil Múinteorí Rincí Gaelacha*: website: www.irishdancingorg.com
10 *Cumann Rince Náisiúnta* (CRN): website: www.crn.ie
11 *Comhaltas Ceoltori Eirean*: website: www.comhaltas.ie
12 *Cumann Rínce Dea Mheasa*: website: www.crdm.ie
13 Ní Bhriain, O, *The Terminology of Irish Dance*.
14 Shoes: Rutherford Shoes: website: www.rutherfordshoes.com
15 Shoes: Antonio Pacelli: website: www.antoniopacelli.com
16 Costumes: 'Eire Designs' by Gavin Doherty: www.gavindoherty.co.uk
17 Headwear: www.paulaswigsandbling.com
18 Make-up: www.readytofeis.com
19 CLRG: *Official Set Dance Handbook*.

20 Francis Ward: private communication.

21 Michael Fitzpatrick: private communication.

22 Ní Bhriain, O, and McCabe, M, *Jigs to Jacobites.*

23 CLRG: *Official Céilí Dance Book.*

24 Mary Kerin: private communication: MDF seminar, UoL, 5–7 July 2013.

25 Michael O'Doherty: private communication: MDF seminar, UoL, 5–7 July 2013.

26 University of Limerick website: www.ul.ie

27 Irish World Academy of Music and Dance: www.irishworldacademy.ie

28 One Dance UK: www.onedanceuk.org

29 Bernadette Flynn: private communication: MDF seminar, UoL, 5–7 July 2013.

30 James Moran: private communication: MDF seminar, UoL, 5–7 July 2013.

31 Peter O'Grady website: irishdancingphysicalfitness.ic

32 British Red Cross website: www.redcross.org.uk

33 St John Ambulance website: www.sja.org.uk

34 HSE risk assessment website: www.hse.gov.uk/risk

INDEX

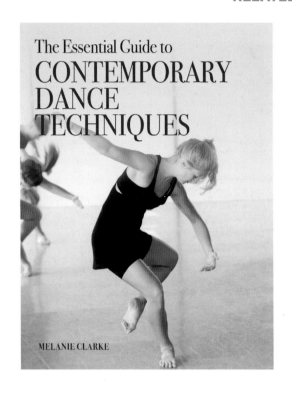

The Essential Guide to
CONTEMPORARY DANCE TECHNIQUES

MELANIE CLARKE

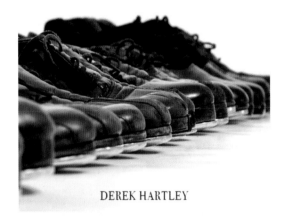

THE ESSENTIAL GUIDE TO
Tap Dance

DEREK HARTLEY

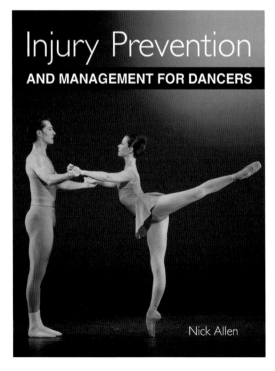

Injury Prevention
AND MANAGEMENT FOR DANCERS

Nick Allen

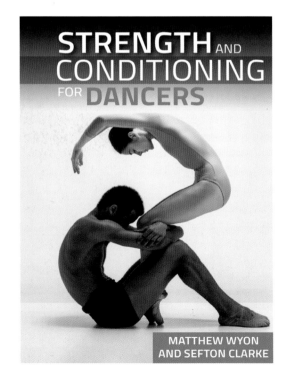

STRENGTH AND **CONDITIONING** FOR **DANCERS**

MATTHEW WYON
AND SEFTON CLARKE